ACCOUNTS

OF THE

GYPSIES OF INDIA

ACCOUNTS OF THE GYPSIES OF INDIA

EDITED BY

DAVID MACRITCHIE

GYAN

Published by

Gyan Publishing House
5, Ansari Road
Daryaganj, New Delhi-110002
Phone: 011-47034999, 9811692060
E-mail: books@gyanbooks.com

Distribution Network
gyanbooks.com
India, USA, Canada, UK, Australia

ISBN: 978-93-6433-478-5 (PB)

First Published, 1886

2nd Impression 2024

Printed at: Gyan Press, Delhi.

ACCOUNTS OF THE GYPSIES OF INDIA
Editor: DAVID MACRITCHIE

ACCOUNTS OF

THE GYPSIES OF INDIA

NOTE.—In this Map the chief places mentioned in Professor De Goeje's treatise are underlined in red.

ACCOUNTS

OF THE

GYPSIES OF INDIA

COLLECTED AND EDITED BY

DAVID MACRITCHIE

AUTHOR OF "ANCIENT AND MODERN BRITONS"

WITH MAP AND TWO ILLUSTRATIONS

LONDON

KEGAN PAUL, TRENCH & CO., 1, PATERNOSTER SQUARE

1886

PREFACE.

"THERE are four hundred books on the gypsies," says a modern *tsiganologue*, "but in all not more than ten which tell us anything new or true about them." Whether this statement is meant to be accepted literally or not, it is evident that much of what is written upon this subject is merely the echo of previous accounts. And also, that a false light has frequently been thrown upon the figures of the gypsies, owing to the fact that they have often been described by people having little or nothing of intimacy with them, and knowing little or nothing of their history. This being so, it is necessary that an addition to the "four hundred" should show good cause why it has come into being.

Nothing in the way of apology requires to be made for the introducing of Professor De Goeje's treatise to English readers; to the most of whom it has the desired qualities of newness and truth. The translation here given has had the benefit of the author's careful revision, and has met with his approval. This was most necessary, as the editor is neither the translator, nor has he any acquaintance with the authorities quoted, nor with the languages in which they wrote. As a study, by an Oriental scholar, of certain passages in the history of an Oriental race, the "Contribution" is unquestionably of value. The same theme had previously been treated of—in 1853, by Dr. Pott, and, earlier still, by M. Paul Bataillard, in 1849—but not with the fullness of research displayed by Mr. De Goeje.

The names of Bataillard and De Goeje,

however, represent two very opposite sides, in certain matters of belief; and it is not inappropriate to remark that, with every respect for the erudition which the "Contribution" displays, its editor does not wholly concur in all the deductions of its learned author. This difference of opinion shows itself in more than one passage in the appended Notes, and elsewhere.

As for the Appendix itself, it is essential to remark that, although explanatory in some degree of several of the allusions in Mr. De Goeje's treatise, it really embodies a good deal of other information. Had this long series of notes been the only thing appended to the "Contribution," forming with it a separate publication, the portentous size of the Appendix would have been an unpardonable offence, to author and to reader. But it seemed convenient to incorporate various other remarks with those which directly relate to the "Contribution;" and in this lies my excuse for the bulk of this Appendix. A like apology must also be offered to the Author, for the expression, in the same place, of more than one sentiment at variance with the opinions which he holds.

The description given of the siege of Bhurtpoor must necessarily appear an excrescence to gypsiologists pure and simple. But it is easy to evade the reading of it. On the other hand, a different class of readers may find more interest in it than in the other portions of the book. It is the former, however, who are chiefly addressed in these pages, and it is hoped that they will find, even in the restatement of various facts well known to them, something that will throw fresh light upon the subject.

CONTENTS.

A CONTRIBUTION

TO THE

HISTORY OF THE GYPSIES.

BY

M. J. DE GOEJE.

(*Extracted from the Proceedings of the "Koninklijke Akademie van Wetenschappen" of Amsterdam*, 1875; *by permission of the Author. From a translation by Mr. J. Snijders, of Edinburgh.*)

SINCE the publication of Pott's book upon the gypsies—about thirty years ago—we have come to regard the origin of this singular people with considerable unanimity of opinion. Almost nobody doubts now that they are Indians; and the assumption that all the gypsies scattered throughout Europe are descended from one parent stock meets with little contradiction. Both of these beliefs are the outcome of the investigation of their language. But, on the other hand, the history of the gypsies, prior to 1417—when they emerged from Hungary and crossed the frontiers of Germany—is almost completely shrouded in darkness. Scattered proofs have been found of their residence, at an earlier date, in the Slavonic countries and in the island of Cyprus, but all else is conjecture. Thus, Grellmann has placed their departure from India in the time of Timur, an idea more fully worked out by Rienzi and Heister, who assume that they were employed by Timur as spies and foragers,[1] and that they were afterwards carried further west by the Turks, in the same capacity. So far as I am aware, this theory has continued to remain a mere supposition unsupported by proof. There is nothing to be found in the history of Timur for or against

[1] This theory is perhaps derived from *Vita Timuri*, Manger's edition, iii. p. 804, *et seq.*, taken in conjunction with i. p. 487. But these passages do not warrant the belief.

it. Others, again, place the gypsy migration in a very remote past. I am not here referring to the exquisite hypothesis which Steur has recently advanced in his *Ethnographie des peuples de l'Europe*,[1] that the gypsies may be the descendants of the dwellers in the sunken Atlantis. But Bataillard[2] is inclined to believe that there is a connection between the *Sicani*, the aboriginal people of Sicily, and the *Zigeuners*[3] (or *Zigani*). He leaves us in doubt, however, as to his reasons for this conjecture, beyond the uniformity in name. I believe I have also seen it stated somewhere that there is a possible connection between the Siculi (Zekel, Sycli) of the Hungarian chronicles and the Zigeuners. The Siculi are certainly

[1] iii. p. 266, *et seq.*

[2] *Revue Critique*, 1870, ii. p. 213; compared with p. 208, note 2.

[3] [Except on such an occasion as this, where it is obviously necessary to retain the original word, I have rendered Mr. De Goeje's *Zigeuner* by our own equivalent, *gypsy*.—Ed.]

described as a race possessing many peculiarities.[1] But then, they had inhabited Hungary for centuries before there can be any question of *gypsies* in that territory. In place of all these conjectural theories, however, I believe I am in a position to communicate certain positive accounts, which I desire to submit to your consideration.

Pott, in the introduction to his book,[2] and quoting from the *Shâh-Nâme* of Firdousi, informs us that, during the fifth century of our era, the Persian monarch, Behram Gour, received from an Indian king 12,000 musicians of both sexes, who were known as Lûrîs. Now, as this is the name by which the gypsies of Persia are known even at the present day, and as, moreover, the author of the Persian work *Modjmal at-tawârîkh*[3]

[1] *Script. rerum Hungar., ed. Schwandtnen, Vindob*, 1746–48, i. pp. 33, 78, 334, (758), 786.

[2] i. p. 62.

[3] See Reinaud, *Mémoire sur l'Inde*, p. 112. As regards the authorities in this book, Reinaud refers to them in

emphatically says that the Lûrìs or Lûlîs of modern Persia are the descendants of these same 12,000 musicians, there is no hazard in the assumption that we have here the first recorded gypsy migration. Confirmation of this is afforded by the Arabian historian, Hamza of Ispahan, who wrote half a century before Firdousi, and who was well versed in the history of the Sassanides. It is related by this author that Behram Gour caused 12,000 musicians, called Zott, to be sent from India for the benefit of his subjects. And *Zott* is the name by which the gypsies were known to the Arabs, and which they even bear in Damascus at the present day. In the Arabic dictionary *al-Kâmûs* this entry occurs: "*Zott*, arabicized from Jatt, a people of Indian origin. The word might be pronounced *Zatt* with equal correctness. A single individual is called *Zottî*." In the

the preface to his *Fragments arabes et persans*, p. vii, *et seq.* See also Elliot, *History of India*, i. p. 100, *et seq.*; ii. p. 161, *et seq.*

lexicon *Mohît* we read: "*Zott*, a race from India, arabicized from Jatt; Zottish clothes are named after them, a single piece being called Zottî. These are the people who are called Nawar in Syria, and sometimes they are styled Motribîya (*i.e.* musicians), their avocation being that of players upon stringed instruments and drums. They are likewise dancers. Their name is also employed as a term of contempt. Thus people say, when they wish to characterize others as *low* or *contemptible*, 'So-and-so is a Zottî,' or, more directly, 'You Zottî!'"[1] Under the heading *Nawar*, the gypsies are described at great length, in terms which recall the type with which we are familiar. Bocthor says, in his French-Arabic dictionary, that "Bohémien" (particularized as "wandering Arab, Tchinghianè, who tells fortunes, steals, etc.") is called at Kesrowân *Nawarî*, plur. *Nawar*, and at Damascus *Zottî*, plur. *Zott*.[2] Lastly,

[1] [See Appendix, Note A., "*Zottî*, a Term of Contempt."]

[2] [See Appendix, Note B., "Arabic and English Plurals."]

Vullers, in his Persian dictionary, quotes this from a native Persian dictionary: "Djat nomen tribus segregatæ infimæ sortis et deserta habitantis in Hindûstân." In the library of Leyden we possess a remarkable little book, as yet unpublished, written about the year 1235 by Jaubarî, entitled *Secrets Revealed,* in which are described all the occupations of the people whom we designate *kermisvolk.*[1] In this book, of which I have given a lengthy account in the twentieth part

[1] [That is, *fair-people;* by which is meant *travelling showmen, mountebanks, acrobats, jugglers, minstrels, fortune-tellers, card-sharpers, thimble-riggers,* and others of that class of itinerant performers, once so conspicuous a feature of the Dutch (as of the British) fair or market. From two subsequent references of Mr. De Goeje's (at pp. 30 and 48), it is evident that he regards those *kermisvolk* as being, or as having been originally, *gypsies* by blood. Mr. C. G. Leland also bears a like testimony, when he says of such people (at p. 140 of *The Gypsies*): "If there be not descent [from the Romané], there is affinity by marriage, familiarity, knowledge of words and ways, sweethearting and trafficking, so that they know the children of the Rom as the house-world does not know them, and they in some sort belong together."—ED.]

of the *Zeitschrift der deutschen morgenländischen Gesellschaft*, the gypsies are again spoken of under this name *Zott*.

For the fatherland of these Zott, or Jatt, we have not long to seek. Istakhri[1] and Ibn-Haukal,[2] the celebrated tenth-century geographers, recount as follows:—"Between al-Mansûra and Mokrân the waters of the Indus have formed marshes, the borders of which are inhabited by certain Indian tribes, called Zott: those of them who dwell near the river live in huts, like the huts of the Berbers, and subsist chiefly on fish and water-fowl; while those occupying the level country further inland live like the Kurds, supporting themselves on milk, cheese, and maize."

In these same regions there are yet two more tribes placed by these geographers, namely, the Bodha and the Meid.[3] The

[1] Page 180 of my edition.

[2] Page 235 of my edition. Mokaddasi gives a similar account to Istakhri.

[3] The pronunciation of both these names is variable.

former are properly, according to Ibn-Haukal,[1] a subdivision of the Zott; or, more correctly, a part of the "country of the Zott" is denominated Bodha. Therefore Belâdsorî[2] speaks also of "the Zott of al-Bodha."[3] Concerning these two tribes we read:[4] "The heathen inhabiting the borders of Sind are the Bodha and a people called the Meid. The former consist of tribes scattered between the frontiers of Tûrân,[5] Mokrân, Multân, and the territory of Mansûra; they dwell to the west of the Indus, and live by camel-rearing. They supply the two-humped camel-stallions,

Thus some manuscripts have *Nodha* for *Bodha*, this spelling being adopted by Yakût; while many other writings have *Mend* instead of *Meid.*

[1] Page 40.

[2] [See Appendix, Note C., "Belâdsorî."]

[3] Page 436, l. 2, of my edition.

[4] Istakhrî, p. 176; Ibn-Haukal, p. 231.

[5] That province of Sind in which Kosdar is situated. [This *Kosdar* appears to be that *Khozdur* which is situated to the west of the frontiers of Sind, and within the territory of Beloochistan. At one time, presumably, the boundaries of Sind had included that portion of modern Beloochistan.—Ed.]

which are sought after all over the East, and from which the celebrated breeds of Balkh and Samarkand are descended. They bring their produce to market at the town of Kandabîl,[1] where also they procure for themselves other necessaries. They are true nomads, living in huts like the Berbers, and finding a safe retreat in their reedy fen lands, where they support themselves by fishing. The Meid dwell along the course of the Indus, from the borders of Multân down to the sea; and the plain stretching between the Indus and Kâmohol affords them many pastures and camping-grounds, winter and summer. They form a large population." A later writer[2] adds to this that they differ little from the Zott. That the Bodha properly belong to the Zott is confirmed by the *Modjmal at-tawârîkh*,[3] wherein it is stated

[1] Not far to the east of Kosdar (Reinaud, *Mémoire*, p. 234); the modern Gandáva (according to Elliot, *History of India*, i. p. 385, *et seq.*).

[2] Yakût, iv. p. 773, l. 3.

[3] Reinaud, *Fragments*, p. 25, *et seq.*

that of old there were only two tribes in Sind, the one called Meid, the other Zott, and both descended from Ham.[1] After the latter of these, says this writer, the Arabs still term this district "the country of the Zott."[2] In course of time, the Meds (to adopt the spelling favoured by Sir Henry Elliot) overcame the Zotts, whom they treated with such severity that they had to leave the country. The Zotts then established themselves on the river Pehen,[3] where they soon became skilful sailors. Next, they began to make piratical raids upon the Meds (who supported themselves by sheep-rearing), until the latter were at length compelled to conclude a treaty with them, by which they agreed to ask from the king a prince who

[1] [See Appendix, Note D., "The Meid or Meds."]

[2] [*Dera-Jat*, that portion of the Punjaub which stretches for fully two hundred miles alongside the course of the Upper Indus, which river forms its eastern boundary.—Ed.]

[3] Elsewhere called the *Beher*. It is, no doubt, a branch or affluent of the Indus.

should govern them both together. Under the sway of this sovereign, Sind became populous and cultivated; and the Zotts and Meds were each assigned a separate territory.

That division of the Meds that dwelt along the coast lived by piracy. They were known as Kork [1] (or Kerks), and their voyages even extended to great distances. In the reign of the Khalif al-Mansûr, in 768, they even penetrated into the Red Sea, and captured Jidda, the port of Mecca.[2] So much dreaded was the very sight of their vessels, called *bârî*, or *bârija*, that by some Arabic authors the name of their ships has been transferred to the pirates themselves.[3] And it is most noteworthy that to this day the gypsies use

[1] See an account of them in Elliot's *History of India*, i. p. 508, *et seq.* [Also Appendix, Note E., "The Kork, or Kerks."]

[2] Tabarî, iii. p. 359; Ibno-'l-Athîr, ed. Tornberg, v. pp. 455 and 466; *Kitâbo-'l-Oyûn*, p. 264 of my edition (Fragmenta Hist. Arabic.): compare Yakût, iv. p. 690, l. 4; Reinaud, *Mémoire*, p. 181.

[3] Bîrûnî, according to Reinaud, *Fragments*, pp. 91 and 120; compare my Glossary to *Belâdsorî*, p. 13.

this word (*baro*) for "a ship."[1] Those divisions of the Zotts living farthest to the north are known as Kikân, and were famed as breeders of horses.[2] It is a strange thing that our geographers make no mention whatever of buffaloes, which must then—as now,[3] and in times still earlier—have constituted the most important part of the flocks and herds of these people. A strong proof, surely, of how little is signified by an *argumentum ex silentio.*

Now, these tribes—some of whom, in all likelihood, existed in earlier times as wandering bands, living in true gypsy fashion (as one may still find them in various parts of India)—require, as hunters and herdsmen, a great extent of territory. And, consequently, they are from time to time compelled, as their numbers increase, to send out successive

[1] Pott, ii. p. 89. Elliot (*History of India*, i. p. 539 *et seq.*) is of opinion that from this word *bârija*, comes our [*i.e.* the Dutch] *barge.* [See Appendix, Note F. "Barge, etc."]

[2] Belâdsorî, pp. 432, 433, and 445.

[3] See Ritter, *Erdkunde*, vii. pp. 173 and 175.

detachments, as happens in other lands among similar people. Where the contiguous countries are badly governed, they are invaded by these detachments, who thereby enlarge the dominion of their race; but when these intruders find themselves confronted by powerful states, then nothing is left to them but to become the servants of the inhabitants. This latter event repeatedly came about during the prime of the Sassanides. Excepting the account of the 12,000 musicians who came into Persia in the reign of Behram Gour,[1] we have, indeed, no direct information in this respect. But, during the wars of the Persians and Arabs in the seventh century, we find in the Persian army numerous regiments recruited from these tribes; who, when the Shah's fortunes began to waver, went over to the side of the Arabs and embraced Islamism, on condition of receiving rank and pay.[2] They joined themselves to

[1] [A.D. 420–448.—ED.]

[2] Belâdsorî, pp. 372–377; Mobarrad, Wright's edition, p. 82, l. 16, *et seq.*; Ibno-'l-Athîr, iii. p. 174.

the Banû-Tamîm, a large number of them settling in Basra. We also learn from the narrative of the rebellion of the Arabs under Abu-Bekr,[1] that companies of the Zotts were settled in Bahrein, at al-Khatt, a town on the sea coast. Nor did the Indians who were thus brought into Western Asia consist only of soldiers, but of whole families, who, with their goods and chattels, had been conveyed to the banks of the Euphrates, with, in all probability, the twofold purpose of occupying the fen lands, and of being at the same time a protection against the Bedouin Arabs. Thus, we read in Belâdsorî[2] that while another Indian tribe, called the Sayâbija, was established before the beginning of Islamism on the sea coasts, the cattle of the Zotts were pasturing in the Tofûf, as the bottom lands of the Euphrates, in the neighbourhood of Babylon, are called. An old canal in the Batîha (*i.e.* the marshes of the Euphrates,

[1] Ibno-'l-Athîr, ii. p. 281.

[2] Page 373, penultimate line.

near Babylon) was known, even for a long time after that, as the Nahro-'z-Zott, or "the Canal of the Zotts."[1] Moreover, there was a colony of Zotts established in Khuzistan. It is true that Dimashkî, a comparatively late geographer, says[2] that these Zotts only came there in the time of Hajjâj, in the beginning of the eighth century; but, on the other hand, Belâdsorî[3] mentions *az-Zott* (a contraction of Haumato-'z-Zott, or Haiyizo'-z-Zott; *i.e.* "Territory of the Zott") as among the districts which were conquered in the reign of Omar.[4] This territory, which is situated between Râmhormuz and Arrajân, and consequently in the direction of Farsistan, retained this name even long after its original inhabitants had disappeared, or at any rate

[1] Yakût, under *Nahr*.

[2] Mehren's edition, p. 179, fourth line from foot of page. The writer is evidently not well informed. The text, moreover, is corrupt (read *wahowa jîlon jâa bihim*).

[3] Page 382. *Cf.* p. 377.

[4] [A.D. 635–644. His conquest of Persia was completed in 642.—ED.]

were no longer recognized as Zotts. This I infer from the fact that Yakût speaks of the place as *Ratt* instead of *Zatt*, erroneously omitting a diacritical point, although he was quite familiar with the name Zatt or Zott. This territory is spoken of by Istakhrî and Ibn-Haukal as being extensive, populous, and rich.

What became of these various colonies after the Arabian conquest, is not known in detail. Many have, no doubt, become arabicized, and in later times one still finds descendants of Zotts who rose to high rank, such as Sarî ibno-'l-Hakam, who became governor of Egypt in 815.[1] But Belâdsorî relates[2] that khalif Moâwia, in the year 669 or 670, brought over several families of the Zotts and *Sayâbija* from Basra to Antioch on the Orontes, and other seaboard towns of Syria.[3] Even so lately as the third century of the Muhammadan era, there was a quarter

[1] Abu-'l-Mahâsin, Juynboll's edition, i. p. 574.

[2] Page 162

[3] Page 376.

in Antioch known as Mahallato-'z-Zott ("the quarter of the Zotts"), while, at the same time, there were Zotts—said to be descendants of these people—living in Bûka, which is within the dominion of Antioch. Here, then, we have the earliest settlement of Zotts in the neighbourhood of the frontiers of the Byzantine Empire.[1]

It was partly on account of the resistance made by the Meds[2] and the Kîkân[3] (as the northmost division of the Zotts was called[4]) that the first invasions of the Arabs into India were unsuccessful. But these tribes were soon convinced of the power of their new enemies. And when, in the beginning of the eighth century, under the khalifate of Walîd I., the Moslems undertook their first serious expedition against India, they found in the Zotts and Meds allies, and not oppo-

[1] [See Appendix, Note G., "Earliest Settlement of Gypsies in Europe."]

[2] Belâdsorî, p. 433.

[3] *Ibid.*, p. 432, *et seq.*

[4] *Ibid.*, p. 445.

nents. The army with which Hajjâj, the governor of Irâk, sent his nephew, Mohammed ibno-'l-Kâsim, to the Indus Valley was not a large one,[1] but it was gradually increased by volunteers from among the Zotts.[2] They did not, however, make very trustworthy allies, and it was therefore resolved that a considerable number of them should be deported. By this proceeding, another and a most necessary end was gained. The Tigris, like the Euphrates, had its stretches of marsh land, especially in Kaskar, an otherwise very rich province lying towards Khûzistân. For the cultivation of these tracts, no more suitable inhabitants could be found than these very Zotts, reared among the marshes of the Indus; while buffaloes, of which their herds mainly consisted, are the only cattle that will thrive in marshy districts.[3]

[1] Belâdsorî, p. 436.

[2] *Ibid.*, p. 438. See also Elliot, *History of India*, i. pp. 161, 187, and 435.

[3] See, for example, Petermann, *Reisen*, ii. p. 423, Remark 31 relating to i. p. 171.

We are told by Belâdsorî[1] that other families from Sind, as well as the Zotts, were conveyed thither, together with their women, children, and buffaloes ; but the Zotts seem to have supplied the main contingent, as the whole colony was named after them. This event must have happened about the year 710. For we read that al-Walîd, who died in 714, caused a part of these Zotts, with their buffaloes, to be transported to Antioch and al-Maççîça. Other relative information[2] gives us also an estimate of the greatness of this deportation. Abu-Nomân of Antioch relates : "The road between Antioch and al-Maççîça (the ancient Mopsuestia) was in old time unsafe on account of wild animals, and more than once a traveller was attacked by a lion. When complaints of this were brought to al-Walîd ibn-Abdo-'l-malik, he sent thither 4000 buffaloes, both bulls and cows, and through these Allah gave deliverance."

[1] Page 375.

[2] Belâdsorî, pp. 162, 167, 168, and 376.

(It is a well-known fact that the buffalo has the courage to withstand the lion.[1]) "For Mohammed ibno-'l-Kâsim at-Thakafî, Hajjâj's vicegerent in Sind, had sent from there several thousands of buffaloes, and of these Hajjâj sent 4000 to Syria—to al-Walîd—whilst he disposed the remainder among the fens of Kaskar. When, after the death of Yazîd ibno-'l-Mohallab, in the year 720, the property of the Mohallabites was confiscated, there were found amongst their possessions 4000 buffaloes in Kaskar and the bottom lands of the Tigris. These were sent by Yazîd II., along with the Zott families connected with them, to al-Maççîça, and thus there were altogether 8000 buffaloes conveyed to that place. During the agitated times of Merwân II., the last khalif of the Omayades, the inhabitants of Antioch and Kinnesrîn appropriated a share of these herds. But when al-Mançûr, the second

[1] See, for instance, Kazwînî, Wüstenfeld's edition, i. p. 883.

khalif of the Abbasides, came to the throne, he commanded them to be returned to al-Maççîça.[1] Thus the buffaloes now found in Antioch and Bûka are descended from those which were brought by the Zotts who had been taken thither by Moâwia and Walîd I."

While thus the first colonies of Zotts were brought into Upper Syria in the reign of Moâwia, a second colony was subsequently sent thither by Walîd I., and this was followed by a third under Yazîd II. Now, as the principal colony remained in Kaskar, we can reckon that the number of Zotts transported thither by Mohammed ibno-'l-Kâsim was very considerable. It is not until the year 820 that we again hear of these.[2] The Zotts had increased greatly in number in these Kaskar lowlands, and had so availed themselves of the state of semi-

[1] This town was rebuilt by al-Mançûr, on account of which it was named al-Mançûra, as we are told by Edrîsî (Jaubert's translation, i. p. 162).

[2] Ibno-'l-Athîr, vi. p. 256 ult.; Abu-'l-Mahâsin, i. p. 590.

anarchy into which the country was cast during the war between the sons of Hârûn ar-Rashîd, al-Emîn and al-Mâmûn, that they had obtained the mastery throughout the regions of the Lower Tigris. Strengthened by runaway slaves and malcontents who had found a refuge amongst them, they were emboldened to take possession of the highways—by land and water—to plunder ships and caravans, and to sack the granaries of Kaskar;[1] whereas formerly, as Belâdsorî relates,[2] the utmost they dared to do was to importune passers-by for alms, and to steal what they could, unnoticed, from passing ships. But now, in 820, matters had reached such a pass that people no longer dared to cross their territory, and ships destined from Basra to Baghdad with provisions remained lying at Basra.

[1] Ibn-Mashkowaih, p. 471 ult., my own edition (Fragm. Hist. Arabic.); and Tabarî, iii. p. 1167, *et seq.* Reinaud has altogether misunderstood the accounts relating to this rebellion (*Mémoire*, p. 200).

[2] Page 375.

The expeditions sent against them by the khalif in 820 and 821 were altogether unsuccessful, with the result that his prestige suffered greatly therefrom. When, in the year 824, submission was demanded, on humiliating conditions, from Naçr ibn-Shabath, an Arab chief who had made himself independent in Syria during the civil wars, he retorted thus: "Shall I consent to this? Can this man imagine he is able to compel the very flower of the Arabs, when he is not even able to bring into subjection some four hundred frogs, who have rebelled under his wing?" By this he signified the Zotts, as the chronicler remarks;[1] but their number greatly exceeded four hundred.

This state of things lasted until 834, when Motacem—who had succeeded Mâmûn—resolved to grapple with the difficulty in earnest. And it was high time, too, as the supply of provisions from Basra to Baghdad

[1] Tabarî (iii. 1069), and after him Ibno-'l-Athîr, vi. p. 275.

was cut off, much to the damage of the khalif's authority. This is shown very clearly from an Arabian satirical poem, composed by a Zott in the time of this rebellion, and communicated to us by Tabarî.[1] From this poem we see that they were, on the one hand, very well informed as to the rebellion in Sind; and that they were equally aware, on the other hand, that the Arabs had a much more formidable enemy to deal with in the mountains of Armenia, namely, Bâbek the Persian. After commiserating the people of Baghdad because they were now deprived of their beloved dates, and then mockingly referring to their finely dressed generals, who were mostly emancipated Turkish slaves, the poet goes on to say how the Zotts will now harass and torment the Baghdadenses (then proceeding against them, "like the real amphibious creatures that they are"), and how they will deal them a blow "that will gladden the lord of Tîz (the capital of

[1] iii. 1169, *et seq.*

Mokrân in Sind), and will cause the lord of the throne[1] (Bâbek the Persian) to laugh with glee." And we further see that as soon as this Zottic insurrection had been quelled, one of Motacem's generals was despatched against their Indian kinsmen.

Thus no time was to be lost in undertaking the subjugation of those Zotts of Kaskar; for which end Ojeif ibn-Anbasa was sent against them with the most unlimited power. A series of post-stations was established between Baghdad and his army, so that the khalif could receive tidings every day, and was thus enabled to send off whatever the general asked for. But it was no easy matter to wage war against those children of the fens. On one occasion only was Ojeif able to force them to give battle, when three hundred of the Zotts were slain, while five hundred more were taken prisoner and afterwards beheaded. Beyond that, it was a series of skirmishes, in

[1] The Sassanidian throne, preserved in Armenia.

which the regular troops were usually the sufferers.

Although Ojeif made every effort to dam up the many canals leading into and out of the fens, he progressed so slowly that not until after the lapse of nine months was he able to bring his enemies to subjection. Bar-Hebræus tells us[1] that, in order to accomplish this, it was necessary to employ certain Egyptian prisoners, accustomed to operate in marshy districts. In the last days of the year 834, the Zotts—on condition that neither their lives nor their possessions were to be forfeited—finally surrendered. Great were the rejoicings at Baghdad! By command of the khalif each soldier of Ojeif's army received a bounty of two *denarii*, and it was ordained that all the Zotts should be brought to the capital and there exhibited to the whole people. It was now seen that their entire number amounted to 27,000, and of these 12,000 were men capable of bearing

[1] At page 153 of the Syrian text.

arms.[1] As the boat-loads of the Zotts, dressed in their national costume, and with their trumpets, passed up the river into Baghdad, the whole populace was ranged along the Tigris banks, and the khalif himself participated in the enjoyment of the spectacle, which he witnessed from his yacht. For three successive days this pageant was enacted. Thereafter, the Zotts were given over to Bishr ibno-'l-Sameida, who conveyed them first to Khanekin (thirty parasangs [112½ English miles] to the north-east of Baghdad), and from there to Ainzarba (Anazarba), on the northern frontier of Syria. Thus runs the narrative of Tabarî. Belâdsorî states[2] that fully the greatest number were taken to Ainzarba, but that a part of them remained in Khanekin, and, moreover, that a few were placed in other parts of the Syrian frontier.[3]

[1] See also Abu-'l-Mahâsin, i. p. 653. [And see Appendix, Note H., "The Zotts in the Valley of the Lower Tigris."]

[2] Page 376.

[3] [See Appendix, Note H., "The Zotts in the Valley of the Lower Tigris."]

We cannot settle with certainty the precise status held by the Zotts when they reached Ainzarba, and their other destinations; yet it is sufficiently clear that they were not received as free citizens. For Wâkidî[1] and Belâdsorî[2] add this remark to their accounts of the deportation to Ainzarba: "and the inhabitants derived much benefit from their services."[3] But this was not to last long.

In the year 855, so says Tabarî, and after him Ibno-'l-Athîr,[4] the Rûm (*i.e.* the Byzantines) made an attack on Ainzarba, when they succeeded in making themselves the masters of all the Zott prisoners in that town. These they carried off with them to their

[1] According to Yakût, iii. p. 761, l. 21, *et seq.*

[2] Page 171.

[3] Ibn-Shihna quotes, in his description of Aleppo (Manuscript Leid. 1444, f. 74 r), the passage from Belâdsorî, adding these words: "I say the Zotts are an Indian people."

[4] Tabarî, iii. p. 1426; Ibno-'l-Athîr, vii. p. 52. Lebeau (*Le bas empire*, xv. p. 87) has erroneously *Aïncarja* for *Ainzarba*.

own country, along with their women, children, buffaloes, and cows.

Here, then, we have the first band of gypsies brought into the Greek Empire.[1] Whether these again were increased by later arrivals from Syria, where there yet remained many Zotts from former deportations, I cannot tell; although this is not at all improbable, as it appears from Jaubarî's book, before referred to, that acrobats, jugglers, and others of that sort also visited Asia Minor from Syria.

Neither can I ascertain whether any deportations of Zotts from India have taken place after the year 710. But it is unlikely, because the chronicles make no mention of such an event, and also because it is only in Syria that the name *Zott* has continued to be the equivalent for *gypsies*.

When the rebellion in Kaskar had been crushed, Sind was attacked in great force,

[1] [See Appendix, Note G., "Earliest Settlement of Gypsies in Europe."]

and speedily subdued. The Zotts and Meds had to suffer severely for it. Those of the former who did not succeed in escaping were each branded on the hand, and a poll-tax was levied on them; while it was further ordained that every man must be provided with a dog, in consequence of which the price of dogs rose to fifty dirhems.[1] The Meds, after having suffered heavy losses in the struggle, had retreated to the marshes of the Indus, where they were joined by the chiefs of the Zotts. The Arab commander then caused a canal to be cut from the sea coast to this marsh, so that the water in it became quite brackish. Thus, the Meds also would soon have been conquered, had it not been for disagreements arising among the Arab rulers, who, as on several previous occasions, broke off the enterprise just on the eve of its completion. The Zotts and the Meds soon

[1] See also Elliot, *History of India*, i. p. 187; and an account of this strange decree, p. 449, *et seq.* Compare Ritter, vii. p. 175.

again returned to their former way of living, and Mas'ûdî, who visited Sind in 915, characterizes them as a torment to the people of al-Mançûra;[1] and they are thus described by Istakhrî and Ibn-Ḥaukal.

In the year 1000, we find bands of Zotts in the army of Abû-Naçr ibn-Bakhtiyâr, in Persia and Kirmân.[2] In 1025, al-Mançûra was conquered by Mahmûd al-Gaznawî, because the prince of this town had forsaken Islamism. From this statement (which is made by Ibno-'l-Athîr[3]), Reinaud infers[4]—and justly, it appears to me—that the Zotts and Meds had here become the ruling race, and had abolished the hated religion of Islam. They themselves had never embraced that religion, for which they were liable, by the law of Islam, to the *jizya*—the head-money exigible from every non-Moslem, in lieu of the death which he strictly merits.

[1] Ed. Barbier de Meynard, i. p. 378.

[2] Ibno-'l-Athîr, ix. p. 114.

[3] ix. p. 243.

[4] *Mémoire*, p. 272.

Reinaud's explanation is rendered all the more probable by the additional statement of Ibno-'l-Athîr, that the king of al-Mançûra, on the arrival of Mahmûd, fled the town and hid himself in the marshes ; and also because of Mirkhond's account, that the Jatts (*i.e.* the Zotts) robbed Mahmûd of a portion of his booty, in retaliation for which he obtained over them a brilliant revenge, though not without great difficulty. They were probably at the same time compelled to embrace Islamism.[1] "By the punishment thus dealt out to them (says Reinaud), the power of the Jatts was broken, though not annihilated. The race continued to increase both in the country and out of it. At the time of Tamerlane's expedition to the north of India, there was a tribe of this name settled in the neighbourhood of Delhi. This tribe maintained itself with great power at the town of

[1] Compare Ritter, vii. p. 179; Elliot, *History of India*, i. pp. 218 and 221, ii. p. 477, *et seq.* [See Appendix, Note I., "Mahmûd's Seventeenth Expedition."]

Bhurtpoor; and after the decay of the Mogul empire, in the latter half of last century, it formed itself into an independent principality. At a later date, it even stood out against the power of the English, and it was only after great exertions that it was subdued. At the present day there are Jatts not only in the valley of the Lower Indus, but also at Kâbûl and in the Sikh territory." [1]

What Reinaud has omitted to mention, or has misrepresented, in this connection is, that the Jauts (Zotts, or Jatts) received a severe punishment at the hands of Timûr. We read in his autobiography [2] that he learned, on coming to a deserted village in the Indus Valley, named Tohâna, that the inhabitants were Jauts, a powerful people, unequalled as thieves and highwaymen. They were Moslems only in name, and plundered travellers and caravans. They were now

[1] [See Appendix, Note J., "The Zotts, Djatts, or Jauts."]

[2] Elliot, *History of India*, iii. p. 428, *et seq.*, 492, *et seq.*

hiding themselves in the swamps and jungles. Two hundred of these Jauts were slain by a detachment of Timûr's army, and many others were taken prisoner, while a great number of their cattle were at the same time captured. But Timûr was further informed that the whole country was disturbed by these Jauts, who were as ants and locusts in number, so he resolved to put a stop for good to their outrages. Accordingly, putting himself at the head of his troops, he led them towards the hiding-place of the Jauts. Two thousand of these "devils," as Timûr calls them, fell in the struggle, and the victor returned laden with booty—consisting of the herds of the Jauts, and their women and children. "And thus," he says, "I freed the land from the plague of the Jauts." I have stated this at some length, because it most distinctly appears that there is no mention of a deportation of Jauts by Timûr, still less that he had any of these people in his service. Immediately after this campaign, he marched to Delhi, and, just before giving battle to the prince of Delhi, he caused 100,000 prisoners —whom he had captured since his arrival in India—to be slaughtered in one day.[1] In the Appendix to the first part of Elliot's *History of India*,[2] we find additional details relating to the Jauts, from which I shall only notice that at present they are very numerous: in Sind they form the majority of the population, and they constitute at least two-fifths of the inhabitants of the Punjaub. The greater part of them are Moslems. In the same Appendix,[3] we find proofs that the Meds also are not, as Reinaud thought, extinct. They still inhabit the district in which the Arabian geographer placed them; but they are no longer so powerful as they once were, and live exclusively by fishing.

Dr. Trumpp gives us some very important statements with regard to those Jauts, in the

[1] Elliot, iii. pp. 436 and 497.

[2] Page 507, *et seq.*

[3] Page 522.

Zeitschrift der deutschen morgenländischen Gesellschaft of 1861.[1] It is his belief that the Jauts, who live along the whole course of the Indus, from the delta up to and within the Peshâwar Valley, are the original Aryan population of the country. They are farmers and camel-breeders, amongst whom certain families of half-savage hunters and fishers wander about. These latter are known as Bhangî (*drunkards*),[2] and Dr. Trumpp[3] says of them that they "always appear to me to be our gypsies." Nowadays they are mostly Moslems, upon whom the Hindus look down with contempt, and thus in the Punjaub the name Jaut has almost become a nickname.[4] Nevertheless, it is evident, from their ancient poems and legends, that there was a time when they occupied a much higher rank. As has been seen, this is fully confirmed by history. Their language, now generally

[1] xv. p. 690, *et seq.*

[2] [See Appendix, Note K., "Bhangi."]

[3] Page 695. [4] [See Appendix, Note A.]

known as Sindhî, still bears the name of *Jat-kî-galî*, or Jat-language, in East Belûchistân and the Western Punjaub. According to Trumpp, it is purer and richer in forms than any other of the newer Indian languages, and stands in a much closer relationship to the ancient Prâkrît.[1] The old Prâkrît grammarians treat it with little respect; but this is presumably the result of the contempt with which the people of the Indus region were, at an early date, regarded by the Hindus, a sufficient explanation of which is given by Trumpp. This scholar has expressed as his opinion, although with some hesitation, that the Jauts are related to the ancient Getæ or Goths.[2]

That there was a connection between the gypsies and these Indian Zotts or Jauts, had

[1] Our fellow-member, Mr. Kern, in a review of Trumpp's *Grammar of the Sindhî Language*, has pronounced this assertion to be in the main correct. See *Bijdragen tot de taal-, land- en volkenkunde van Ned. Indië*, 1873, p. 367, *et seq.*

[2] [See Appendix, Note L., "Jauts and Goths."]

already been advanced as a feasible theory by Pott, in the *Zeitschrift* of 1853,[1] wherein he, among other things, repeats various statements obtained from Fleischer. Not the least remarkable of these is the Arabian proverb, which we receive from Meidânî, who wrote about A.D. 1100[2]: "You needn't teach a detective how to make investigations, or a Zott how to commit a theft"—to which may be added,[3] "He is a greater liar than an imprisoned Sindî." To the first proverb the collector adds a note that the Zotts are a low people; and to the second, that every common Sindî gives himself out to be a king's son. By the name Sindî, which the gypsies brought with them to Germany,[4] they were sometimes also indicated in the East; witness Ibn-Batûta, iv. p. 412 of the Paris edition,

[1] vii. p. 393.

[2] Freytag's edition, ii. p. 580, n. 609.

[3] ii. p. 381, n. 211.

[4] [Mr. De Goeje (referring to *Lallemant*, iv. 174) further remarks: "In the German Argot the gypsies are known also by the name of *Sente*."—ED.]

in which the words translated "*à la façon des natifs du Sind*" must be read "*à la façon des Bohémiens.*"[1] See also the *Vocabulista in Arabico*, Schiaparelli's edition, in which *sindî* is rendered by *mimus*,[2] while in the Latin-Arabic part *sindî* is one of the definitions of *mimus in instrumentis*. Another name given them here is *dozdokî*, which is derived from the Persian *dozd*, and, like it, signifies *thief*—a characteristic name for gypsies. It is most likely their fault that their former compatriots came into such bad odour that Vullers, under *dozdî* (theft), quotes the Persian by-word, "A theft by a Hindu is nothing wonderful;" which saying is used when a low and mean man commits a disgraceful act. Worse still, we read under *Hindû* that this word is used appellatively with the signification of *thief*.

In connection with all this, the passage in

[1] My attention has been directed to this passage, as also to that in the *Vocabulista*, by our fellow-member, Mr. Dozy.

[2] [See Appendix, Note M., "Mimus."]

Meidânî is another proof in addition to those already given, that the Zotts of Western Asia are really gypsies. The name *Zott*, however, is only used in Damascus nowadays to denote those gypsies who rear cattle,[1] although every one knows them to be of the same origin as the gypsies who are engaged in other industries, and who are known by other names. In Persia they still bear the name of Lûrî or Lûlî, applied to them long ago by Firdousi. Ouseley relates[2] that they are well aware that their kinsmen are called Tchingâni by the Turks. The name Lûrî does not properly belong to them, but is probably only one of the many names given to this people in consequence of false theories regarding their origin. The Persians seem to have taken them to be natives of Lûristân, which people must bear some resemblance to gypsies in their external appearance.[3] It

[1] See Wetzstein in the *Zeitschrift*, xi. p. 482.

[2] *Travels*, iii. p. 401.

[3] [May it not be that Lûristân received its name

is, however, noteworthy that the gypsies of Egypt are also called Lûrîs in the work entitled *Masâlik al-abçâr*,[1] written in 1337. Saladdîn is said to have caused a great number of them to be put to death. In Transoxania, during the sixteenth and seventeenth centuries, they are called Lûlî.[2] On account of their dark complexion they are sometimes regarded as Africans, and called Zendjîs. For example, the Persian translator of Istakhrî has sometimes written Zengiân in the text, instead of Zotts.[3] In Persia, at the present day, they are also often called Berbers, and thus confounded with the North Africans. They have often acquiesced in the appellation *Egyptians*, given to them

because it was originally peopled by Lûrîs, or gypsies, who would thus be best entitled to be styled "natives of Lûristân?"—Ed.]

[1] *Notices et Extraits*, xii. p. 330, *et seq.*

[2] Abu-'l-Ghâzî, *Histoire des Mongols*, par Desmaisons pp. 258, 259, 276, and 282.

[3] As on page 35 of my edition. Compare Reinaud, *Mémoire*, p. 273, note 3, and Pott, i. p. 45, *et seq.*

in Europe: in the East, so far as I am aware, that name does not occur—any more than the name Rom'ni, which they apply to themselves, and justly, since it signifies "men."[1]

As regards the destinies of the Zotts after they had been brought to Asia Minor from Ainzarba, in the year 855, I have been unable—in the course of a hurried search—to discover anything. But, now that we know the year in which they entered Byzantine territory, others may be more successful. Whether the name Zott, or rather its Indian form Jat (or Jaut), has also been brought with them into Europe, I am, of course, as little able to say. In the Appendix to the first part of Elliot's *History of India*, I find the following remarkable passage:[2]—"We have undoubted proofs that Indian troops were raised and sent to take part in the battles of the Arabs in distant

[1] [See Appendix, Note N., "Rom, Rom'ni, etc."]

[2] Page 465.

states. I do not speak here of the many Jats in Irâk, Syria, and Mesopotamia, who—as I hope to show before long in another place—were soon changed into the Jatano or Gitano, the gypsies of modern Europe. These had been too long settled by that time in their various colonies, to be spoken of as 'Sindians' by a contemporary writer, such as Dionysius Telmarensis, who was more familiar with the terms 'Jat,' 'Asâwira,' and 'Sabâbija.' But this author, in his Syrian chronicle, definitely mentions 'Sindian' cohorts as forming a part of the greatly mixed army that invaded the Byzantine territory in the year 767." From these words, of which I had no knowledge until this article was almost completed, it appears that the learned author had already seen that the gypsies are descended from the Jauts. The promised treatise, wherein their transformation was to be demonstrated, does not seem to have been forthcoming. But from the combination Zott, Asâwira, and Sabâbija (read Sayâbija), it follows that he only thought of the Zotts, who had been carried away from their fatherland in the days of the Sassanides. The Asâwira were probably, like these, foreign troops in the Persian service, though not Indians. Thus the great deportation of 820 was presumably unknown to him. But his supposition that the old name yet survives in *Gitano* is very weak; for it is only in Spain that the gypsies are thus called, and it is, I think, beyond a doubt that here the name signifies "Egyptian," the name by which they are known in many other countries.[1]

The Indian name, out of which the Arabs made Zott, is Jat with soft *j*, which by non-Indians is sometimes rendered by *z*, sometimes by *j*. The *t* is hardened to *teth* by the Arabs.[2] Yakût mentions also the pronunciation *Zatt* with *a*, which is given in

[1] [See Appendix, Note O., "The Egyptians or Gitanos."]

[2] [*Teth*, according to Dutch orthoepy; *tt* in English. —Ed.]

the *Kâmûs* as the regular pronunciation. But the usual sound is that of *Zott* with *o*, which Bar-Hebræus even lengthens to *û*, as he writes *Zûtojo*. In India the pronunciation *Jut* also occurs.

On the other hand, the gypsies have brought the name Sindî to Germany,[1] thereby preserving the memory of their fatherland. I have also brought under your notice the fact that their word for *ship* is that which their ancestors more than a thousand years ago applied to the vessels in which they undertook their piratical voyages from the Indus mouths. There is yet another word to which I must call attention. The gypsies call a Christian *Gandorry*,[2] a term which seems to be derived from *Gandâra*, the name of a town of such great importance in those regions that its coins, as Ibn-Haukal states,[3] were commonly used in Sind.

[1] Pott, i. p. 33, *et seq.* [See *ante*, p. 39, note [4].]

[2] Pott, ii. p. 125.

[3] Page 228, l. 14. The Arabs call this town Kandohâr

There is no name with regard to which more explanations have been attempted, and which has led to more false theories as to the origin of these wanderers, than their name of Zigeuner, which, in many different forms, occurs in various countries of Europe and in the Turkish Empire, as well as in Egypt and Syria. I dare not venture to assert that I have discovered the solution of the riddle, but I shall nevertheless offer for your consideration a couple of attempts at an explanation. I have already mentioned those wandering tribes who dwell among the Jauts of Sind, and are surnamed *Banghî.* These have yet another name, that of *Shikârî*, which properly signifies *hunters.* It may be that in early times the Jauts had so named this wandering and despised division of their tribe, and had themselves brought the name

or Kondohâr, which must not be confounded with the modern Kandahar. Compare Reinaud, *Mémoire*, pp. 156 and 196, and Elliot, i. p. 445, with Belâdsorî, p. 445. My friend Mr. Kern, to whose judgment I submitted the above, had no objection to make against it.

westward. The difference between sedentary Jauts, who engage in agriculture and particularly in cattle-rearing, and the wandering Zigeuners (or Zigani), who earn their livelihood as musicians, fortune-tellers (*waarzeggers*, lit. *soothsayers*), jugglers (*goochelaars*), acrobats, and pedlars, is even now very noticeable in Syria, and the first only—the sedentary class—still bears the ancient name *Zott*. In Turkey, also, according to Paspati,[1] the gypsies are even at the present day divided into sedentary and nomadic families, the former of whom look down upon the latter. We may assume that many nomadic families were included in the Jaut deportation, since it is especially in this class that we again find the gypsy type so familiar to us. Thus, the Jauts may have continued as formerly to apply the contemptuous name of *Shikârî* to their nomadic class, this name becoming eventually applied to all Zigeuners (*Zigani*). I can, however, adduce nothing to

[1] *Revue Critique*, 1870, ii. pp. 280–283.

establish this theory, and have, indeed, some doubts as to whether all the forms in which the name Zigeuner occurs will permit of a derivation from Shikârî. This difficulty is even more strongly felt in deriving the name from Shâkara,[1] a town situated on one of the outlets of the Indus, in the territory of those sea-rovers whom we have learned to know under the name of Kork (Kerks). It certainly appears that these people were also called Sangârs or Sangâns, perhaps after the name of this town.[2]

As gypsies have always been famous for their musical talents, and as they must also have speedily made themselves known as musicians in the Byzantine Empire, to translate *Zigeuner* as "musician" would be to take an explanation lying ready to hand, and one also which has superior recommendations to the others. Indeed, the Persian word

[1] Elliot, i. p. 397, *et seq.* Reinaud, *Mémoire*, p. 215. *Cf.* Elliot, p. 508, *et seq.*

[2] Elliot, p. 430; Pott, i. p. 46.

tcheng denotes a sort of harp or cither, much used in the East,[1] and *tchengî* is still, as in earlier times, a common word in Persia and Turkey for "musician," and also for "dancer." In this word *tchengî*, the *î* is properly the Arabic termination of the *nomen relativum*, but it can also be regarded as the Persian termination of the *nomen unitatis*. According to this conception, the word *tcheng*, denoting *the dancer*, *the musician*, may be used as the specific name, and from it, by adding the Persian termination *ân*, the plural *tchengân* would be formed, analogously to *merd* (man or mankind) as the name of the species, *merdî* (a man, an individual), *merdân* (men). The sole question is whether *tchengî* has indeed been thus conceived, and consequently whether *tcheng* occurs in the signification indicated. For the answer to this I am indebted to my friend Mr. Dozy, who

[1] Arabic *çenj*, which is also used for *senj* (cymbals or tambourine). [See Appendix, Note P., "Gypsies as Musicians."]

has directed me to an example in the *Arabian Nights* (vol. iv. p. 694, l. 9 from foot of page), and the explanation of the word by Lane, in his translation of this work (iii. p. 730, n. 22). Thus, in the Byzantine Empire, the name *tchengân*, originally denoting the occupation of these people, must have become eventually applied to them as a proper name. For it follows the gypsies from there to the west of Europe, being afterwards carried eastward by the Turks into Asia. We find in the Turkish Empire, in Europe as well as in Asia and Egypt, *Tchengân*, or *Tchengâne*,[1] with a new plural formation (see Hélot), given as a name of the Zigeuners alternatively with *tchengî*, which, as already stated, signifies musician or dancer. It is said that in Turkey at the present day *tchengâne* signifies also "organ-grinder,"[2] as

[1] The Turks, according to a law of their language, pronounce it Tchingiane. See Paspati, as quoted in the *Revue Critique* of 1870 (ii. p. 287); Bocthor under *Bohémien;* and Pott, ii. p. 45.

[2] Pott, i. p. 45, note.

an *appellativum;* but perhaps this is an application of the name of the people to the occupation itself.

There is much in favour of this explanation, but it is difficult to say whether the *n* in the first syllable of the name is original or not. Bataillard is decidedly of opinion that it is not. In the second syllable, the *n* alternates with *r*, and it is likewise difficult to say which of these two letters is the original. The sibilant with which the name commences is in nearly all the forms hard, and on that ground Pott rightly rejected[1] the explanation from the word *Zendjî* (a negro).[2]

Let us now consider to what extent the results of the linguistic research agree with the historical data. I have already stated at starting that there is as good as universal agreement upon two points, amongst scholars

[1] i. p. 46.

[2] [See Appendix, Note Q., "Zigeuners, Zigani," etc.]

who have made a serious study of the gypsies: these are, that their fatherland is to be sought in India, and that at least the bands scattered over Europe are all members of one and the same family. The first of these statements has been more fully elaborated, by Pott and Ascoli in particular. According to the former, the gypsy language is closely akin to the dialects of the north-west of India; while the latter takes the gypsies to be Sindîs who have lived for a long time in Afghanistan. Both results direct us to the Valley of the Indus, that is, to the country which has for centuries been inhabited by the Jauts. The second of these two points has been made clear—notably by Paspati and Bataillard. Not only is there a Slavonic element common to all the gypsy dialects of Western Europe, but they have also (along with those of the Slavonic countries and the Turkish Empire) many Greek words. It follows from this, beyond dispute, that all the gypsies (of Europe) lived for a time upon Greek soil. But a very important addition has to be made to this. That Arabic words should be found in the language of the gypsies of Turkey is no wonder, since Turkish is so very much imbued with Arabic elements. But if these words are also found among the gypsies of Western Europe, who had already inhabited Hungary and Transylvania long before the Turkish conquest of the Danube Provinces, there is no other conclusion possible than that the gypsies have also lived collectively in an Arabian country. This must have been before their residence in the Byzantine Empire. Of itself, this is already probable, but it is confirmed by the fact that the number of Arabic words is much smaller than that of Greek words. Though I have only superficially examined the recurrence of Arabic words, I can point out some which are above all question, as *choro* (deep), which occurs in all the gypsy dialects, and also as a noun (depth), see Pott, ii. p. 164, and

Liebich's Glossar, and which must be the Arabic *ghôr; kotor, gotter* (a piece, or bit), Pott, p. 164, and Liebich, which is the Arabic *kot'a; handako* (a furrow, a moat or ditch) Liebich, Arab. *chandak; mochton* (a box) Liebich, the Arabian jugglers' word *moshtân*[1]; *tschâro, szahro, szahn* (dish), Pott, p. 198, *et seq.*, and Liebich, the Arabic *çahn; agor* (end), Pott, p. 45, Arab. *âchir; alicati* (time), Pott, p. 59, Arab. *al-wakt, al-ikât; câha* (house), Pott, p. 91, Arab. *kâha* or perhaps *kâch; kesz* (silk), Pott, p. 119, Arab. *kazz; jar* and *car* (heat), Pott, pp. 125 and 171, Arab *harr.* These words all occur in European gypsy dialects, and can undoubtedly be increased by earnest investigation; but, such as they are, they sufficiently establish the theory that all the gypsies (of Europe) have lived for a time among Arabic-speaking people. It is doubtful whether we can attain

[1] See my article upon Jaubarî in the *Zeitschrift der deutschen morgenländischen Gesellschaft*, xx. p. 506, *et seq.*

farther, at the present stage of gypsiology. Baudrimont, who has written a pamphlet on the gypsies of the Basque country, says,[1] after Bataillard: "I have been led, by various indications, to suspect that the gypsies lived for a long time in Mesopotamia, more particularly in the neighbourhood of Babylon." He does not specify those indications, but as he adds, "and that they became wanderers in consequence of the destruction of this town," it is probable that he had in view something resembling the discovery which De Saulcy believed he had made, which was, that only the gypsy language supplied the explanation of a word in the so-called Median or Scythian cuneiform inscriptions. If that is the case, then Baudrimont's assumption has no value, although it is nevertheless remarkably confirmed by history, as the gypsies have dwelt in those regions for more than a century.

After the historical explanations supplied

[1] *Revue Critique*, 1870, ii. p. 204.

by the Arabian historians, the wild conjectures regarding the gypsies will surely be put an end to. I do not think it necessary to state these, or to combat them, because in the cases in which they have been advanced by able men, such as Bataillard, he and such as he will be the first to retract them. There is, perhaps, only one difficulty that will be left to these scholars, and that is the question whether all the gypsy bands scattered throughout Europe have descended from a troop of over twenty thousand gypsies brought into the Byzantine Empire in the year 855. I cannot, of course, answer this question any better or more fully than those who put the question.

It is not impossible, in the first place, that the gypsies in the Greek Empire had repeatedly received additions from Syria. Moreover, there were gypsy settlements in other frontier towns, and the Byzantines have conquered many of these, especially in the tenth century. There may also have been many voluntary emigrations of gypsies from Syria. In the second place, it is almost certain that in the countries where they have halted for a time they have assimilated other elements to them. Finally, I may point to the Jews, so often compared with the gypsies, amongst whom there exists the same feature of great increase under oppression, and perhaps even in a stronger measure.

But *the* test must be—a comparative study of the different gypsy dialects, according to the rules laid down by Bataillard, in order that, on the one hand, we may have brought together the original vocabulary, divested of foreign elements; and that, on the other hand, we may deduce from the consideration of these elements in what regions the gypsies have successively dwelt, an estimate which has hitherto been only partially made. Thereafter, a comparison of the language of the gypsies with the Sindhî, the speech of the Jauts. And, lastly, a comparison of the gypsy songs and stories with the poems and legends of their Indian kindred, which, as Trumpp assures us,[1] are very numerous—so numerous that he has himself collected twelve volumes of them.

[1] *Zeitschrift*, xv. p. 693.

APPENDIX TO PROFESSOR DE GOEJE'S TREATISE.

NOTE A.—"*Zottî*," *a Term of Contempt.*

Captain R. F. Burton, in his *History of Sindh* (pp. 246, 247: London, 1851), states that "in the eastern parts of Central Asia, the name Jat [*i.e.* *Zottî*] is synonymous with thief and scoundrel." And, in the Notes relating to the chapter (chap. ix.) in which these words occur, he makes the following additional remarks:—

"Jat^u in the Sindhi dialect means, (1) a camel-driver or breeder of camels; (2) the name of a Beloch clan.

"Jat^u, or, written as it is pronounced, 'Dyat^u,' has three significations: 1. The name of a tribe (the Jats). 2. A Sindhi, as opposed to a Beloch—in this sense an insulting expression. So the Belochis and Brahnis of the hills call the Sindhi language 'Jathki.' 3. A word of insult, a 'barbarian;' as in the expression, Do-dasto Jat^u, 'An utter savage.'"

NOTE B.—*Arabic and English Plurals.*

The formation of the singular and plural of words of the class to which *Zottî* (plur. *Zott*) belongs, seems so perverse to those of us who are not Orientalists, that we inevitably Europeanize their terminations. Thus this name becomes, in English, *Zott* or *Jāt* in the singular (though this is really the *plural* form), and the plural is formed in the ordinary way by adding *s*. With the exception of a few instances at the beginning of Mr. De Goeje's treatise, I have ventured to render his plural "Zott," etc., into "Zotts," etc.

Similarly, I have followed Elliot and others in speaking of the tribe of "the Meds," rather than "the Meid;" and also "the Kerks," instead of "the Kerk, or Kork."

NOTE C.—*Belâdsorî.*

Regarding this historian, so often quoted by the author, we learn from Elliot's *History of India* (vol. i. pp. 113 and 115) that he was—

"Ahmad bin Yahya, bin Jábir, surnamed also Abú Ja'far and Abú-l Hasan, but more usually known as Biládurí, who lived towards the middle of the ninth century of our era, at the court of the Khalif Al Mutawakkal, where he was engaged as instructor to one of the princes of his family."

It is further stated that "he was called Biláduri or Bilázurí [otherwise Beládsorí and Balúdsorí], from his addiction to the use of an intoxicating electuary made from the Balázar, or Malacca bean." Thus the name by which he is best known is merely a surname, or *sobriquet;* as though De Quincey were handed down to posterity as *The Opium-Eater*, and no more.

NOTE D.—*The Meid, or Meds.*

The following remarks, relating to the Meid, or Meds, occur in Elliot's *India*[1] (vol. i. pp. 508, 519, 522, and 525):—

"We find the Meds frequently mentioned by the Arab authors on Sind, and, together with their rivals the Jats [or Zotts], they may be considered the oldest occupants of that province, who, in their names as well as persons, have survived to our own times.

"The first account we have of them is in the *Mujmalu-t Tawárikh.* That work mentions that the Jats and the Meds are reputed to be descendants of Ham, the son of Noah, and that they occupied the banks of the Indus in the province of Sind. The Meds, who devoted themselves to a pastoral life, used to invade the territories of the Jats, putting

[1] *The History of India*, edited from the posthumous papers of the late Sir H. M. Elliot, K.C.B., by Professor John Dowson. London, 1869.

them to great distress, and compelling them to take up their abode on the opposite side of the river; but, subsequently, the Jats, being accustomed to the use of boats, crossed over and defeated the Meds, taking several prisoners and plundering their country."

Professor Dowson (vol. i. p. 508) informs us that—

"When the Muhammadans first appeared in Sindh, towards the end of the seventh century, the *Zaths* and *Meds* were the chief population of the country. But as I have already shown that the original seat of the *Med* or *Medi* colony was in the Panjab proper, I conclude that the original seat of the *Iatii*, or Ját colony, must have been in Sindh."

Sir Henry Elliot also says (vol. i. p. 525):—

"We may even extend our views to a still more remote period, and indulge in speculations whether this tribe may not originally have been a colony of Medes. There is nothing in the distance of the migration which would militate against this supposition, for Herodotus mentions the Sigynnæ, as a colony of the Medes settled beyond the Danube: 'How they can have been a colony of the Medes,' he observes, 'I cannot comprehend; but anything may happen in course of time.' The Medians are also said to have accompanied the expedition of Hercules, when he crossed over from Spain into Africa."

This theory of Elliot's, that the *Meds* were

descended from the historic *Medes*, is not at all at variance with Bataillard's beliefs. For the latter is strongly of opinion that the gypsies of Europe (*Tsigani*) are connected with those *Sigynnæ* whom Herodotus reports as settled beside the Danube; and the French *tsiganologue* also informs us that the same idea had occurred to Fernandez de Córdova, a Spanish writer of the year 1615. Now, Herodotus says that the Danubian Sigynnæ were Medes by descent. And thus the gypsies of Europe and the Meds of Sind are respectively traced back to the more ancient Medes, which leaves us to infer that the ancient Medes were of the gypsy race; since various writers pronounce both these divisions of their descendants (or hypothetical descendants) to be families of gypsies.

In which connection, it is interesting to refer back to De Goeje's citation of Baudrimont, Bataillard, and De Saulcy (at p. 56 of the foregoing "Contribution"), and to De Saulcy's suggested connection between the language of the Zigani and the cuneiform writings ascribed to the Medes.

As to the tradition recorded in the *Mujmalu-t Tawáríkh*, "that the Jats and the Meds are reputed to be descendants of Ham," this also is duplicated in Europe. In his article on "Gypsies" in the *Encyclopædia Britannica* (9th edit.), Mr. F. H. Groome quotes the following passage "from the *Itinerarium Symonis Simeonis* (ed. by J. Nasmith,

Cambridge, 1778), where Fitz-Simeon, a Franciscan friar of Dublin, describing his stay in Crete in 1322, says:—'We there saw a people living outside the city (of Candia), who worship according to the Greek rite, *and declare themselves of the race of Ham.*'" And these people are assumed, on various grounds, to be gypsies. Moreover, in Mr. Bataillard's latest utterance (*Les Gitanos d'Espagne et les Ciganos de Portugal:* Lisbon, 1884), he talks of "*la race chamitique* dont je suis convaincu que les Tsiganes font partie;" and this is a belief which, for other reasons, he has held for many years. "Je ne puis douter en effet," he says (*Les Origines*, etc., p. 27), "que les Tsiganes ne soient des Chamites, et plus particulièrement des Kouschites, qui auraient vécu sous les Aryas dans la région de l'Indus assez longtemps pour perdre leur langue kouschite et adopter une langue aryenne, mais dont les premières et très-probablement les plus importantes émigrations vers l'Occident remonteraient cependant à une antiquité très-reculée."

NOTE E.—*The Kork, or Kerks.*

"Under the government of Muhammad ('son of Hárún, son of Zará' al Namarí'), the king of the Isle of Rubies[1] sent, as a present to Hajjáj, certain Muhammadan girls who had been born in his

[1] Ceylon: "so denominated because of the beauty of the women" (Elliot, vol. i. pp. 118, 119).

country, the orphan daughters of merchants who had died there. The king hoped by this measure to ingratiate himself with Hajjáj; but the ship in which he had embarked these girls was attacked and taken by some barks (*bawárij*) belonging to the Meds of Debal:" elsewhere spoken of as "pirates."

* * * * * *

"The pirates, whose insolence [just referred to] led to the final subjugation of Sind, are stated, by a very good authority, to be of the tribe of Kerk, Kruk, Kurk, Karak, or some name of nearly similar pronunciation. . . . M. Reinaud . . . informs us that, in the annals of the Arabs, the Kurk are more than once spoken of as desperate pirates, carrying their expeditions even as far as Jidda, in the Red Sea." After indicating the Indus delta as their probable home at this period, the writer goes on to suggest as extremely likely, that "the north-eastern shores of the Euxine sea" were inhabited by these people so early as the time of Herodotus. He cites many topographical names which appear to embody both *Kerk*, etc., and *Sindi*, etc., and then continues thus:—

"The old reading of the passage in Herodotus, where the Sindi are mentioned (iv. 28), was originally Indi, but commentators were so struck with the anomaly of finding Indians on the frontiers of Europe, and they considered it so necessary to reconcile the historian with geographers, that they have now unanimously agreed to read Sindi, though the reading is not authorized by any ancient manuscripts. It is impossible to say what is gained by the substitution; for Sindi must be themselves Indians, and the difficulty is in no way removed by this arbitrary conversion. Hesychius, moreover—no mean authority—says that the Sindi of the Euxine were, in reality, Indians; nay, more, though writing two centuries before our Kerks are even named or alluded to, expressly calls the Kerketæ [of the Black Sea] also 'an Indian nation.'

"It has been remarked, that even if no such direct testimony had been given, the hints that remain to us concerning the character and manners of these Sindi, the peculiar object of their worship, and their dissolute religious rites and sorceries, would leave no doubt as to the country from which they were derived.

"It is from this region that the Indian merchants must have sailed who were shipwrecked in the Baltic, and presented by the king of the Suevi, or of the Batavi, to L. Metellus Celer, the pro-consul of Gaul; for they could not have been carried round from the continent of India to the north of Europe by the ocean. Various solutions of this difficulty have been attempted. It has been surmised that they might have been Greenlanders, or mariners from North America, or even painted

Britons [who, it ought to be remembered, were styled 'Moors' by the poet Claudian, and whose complexion was 'as black as an Ethiopian's,' according to Pliny.—Ed.]; but the fact cannot be disputed, that they are called plainly 'Indians,' by all the authors who have recorded the fact, however improbable their appearance in those regions might have been."

* * * * * *

"We may here make a passing allusion," Elliot proceeds to say, on the next page, "to another memorial of Indian connection with these parts. The southern neighbours of these Euxine Sindi were the Kolchians. C. Ritter, in his *Vorhalle*, . . . asserts that they came originally from the west of India. Pindar and Herodotus both remark upon the darkness of their complexion. The latter also mentions that they were curly-headed. He states that he had satisfied himself, not only from the accounts of others, but from personal examination, that they were Egyptians, descended from a portion of the invading army of Sesostris, which had either been detached by that conqueror, or, being wearied with his wandering expedition, had remained, of their own accord, near the river Phasis. He also mentions the practice of circumcision, the fabrication of fine linen, the mode of living, and resemblance of language, as confirmatory of his view of an affinity between these nations."

The mode in which Elliot reconciles the apparently diverse origins assigned to these people by the writers to whom he refers is, that the terms "Ethiopia" and "India" were very frequently used by those early authors in a loose and almost interchangeable fashion; and that, consequently, the Kolchians might have been "Ethiopians" (if not "Egyptians"), and yet "Indians."

After other remarks, chiefly topographical, relating to the above paragraphs, he finally says—

"But even allowing that all these miscellaneous instances of resemblance [in the names of places] . . . are indeed purely fortuitous, . . . still it is impossible to yield the Sindi, the Kerketæ, or even the Maidi, to the cavils of an illiberal and hostile spirit of criticism, for, with respect to them, it must be confessed by all but the most obstinately sceptical, that they, at least, stand boldly and prominently forth, as undoubted evidences of actual Indian occupancy on the shores of the Euxine." [And this once admitted, then the topographical evidence, or the bulk of it, ought also to be accepted, as a *result* of the known presence, in that neighbourhood, of tribes bearing such-and-such names.]

NOTE F.—*Barge, etc.*

Sir Henry Elliot comments upon this word (*History of India*, vol. i. pp. 539, 540), as follows:—

"The term used by Biláduri to represent a vessel of war is *Bárija.* He uses the same word, in the plural, in speaking of the vessels which were captured by the Meds, on their voyage from Ceylon to the Persian Gulf, an act of piracy which led to the Arab conquest of Sind."

"Bírúní says also, a century later, that the *Bawárij* are established at Kachh and Somnát, and are so called because they devote themselves to the pursuit of piracy, in ships which are called *Bera.* . . . This is a native word still in use for a boat, but the origin of the term *Bawárij* must be sought, not in the Indian *Bera*, but rather in the Arabic *Bárija*, which Golius, on the authority of the *Kámús*, tells us to mean a large vessel of war.

"From the same source our English *Barge* seems to be derived. . . ."

And so on. It is unnecessary, however, to follow Elliot in all his remarks upon the etymology of this word. Especially when he says, "But we have no occasion to look for any connection between our words *Bark* and *Barge.* The former is confessedly an old word, the latter comparatively modern." There is practically no difference between English *bark*, or *barque*, and Dutch *barge*, (*g* hard), Low-Latin *barga*, Latin *barca*, etc. And the soft sound of the *g* in our modern *barge* is a transition which has many parallels in English. An additional statement by Mr. De Goeje, that the Arabic writer,

Mokaddasî, pronounces the word as *bêrga*, indicates also a like approximation in the East.

The opinion held by various etymologists, that all these forms are derived from the root *ber*, to carry or *bear*, is surely incontrovertible. Thus the word originally meant "something that bears, or carries." And, when gypsies speak of a ship as *baro*, they are merely employing in a nautical sense the word which in modern English is restricted to a more humble kind of "vessel," used only by "navigators" of the land, viz. *barrow*.

NOTE G.—*Earliest Settlement of Gypsies in Europe.*

When Mr. De Goeje speaks of the "earliest settlement" of gypsies on the confines of the Byzantine Empire, and (not long after) on the confines of Europe, he of course signifies the earliest settlement *recognized as such by him*. But it does not follow that such a settlement was actually "the earliest." This is frequently pointed out by Mr. Bataillard (*e.g. L'origine des Tsiganes*, p. 29, *et seq.*: Paris, 1877), whose ideas, in this respect, are diametrically opposed to the opinions of Mr. De Goeje. Indeed, as far back in time as there was a recognizable gypsy type, so far back may there have been gypsy migrations to or from any part of the world.

NOTE H.—*The Zotts in the Valley of the Lower Tigris.*

Whether these insurgents were mainly descended from the colonists of the year 710, or whether their numbers had been very largely increased by the "runaway slaves and malcontents," to whom reference is made, it is clear from the figures quoted that the khalif's army had a most formidable foe to encounter. "Twelve thousand men capable of bearing arms" could well dominate the two or three hundred miles between Baghdad and Bussorah; and their numbers were virtually doubled by the fact that the campaign was conducted in a swampy region, with which they were all familiar, while the tactics required in such a warfare had been practised by them and their forefathers for many generations. The Arab chief fell far short of the truth when he alluded to them as "four hundred frogs."

That this insurrection was largely the uprising of a *race* (in spite of the heterogeneous refugees), may be seen from their wearing a *national* garb; and this may also be inferred from their knowledge of, and sympathy with, the contemporaneous rebellion of the Zotts of Sind—which is shown by the Zottic satirical poem referred to by Mr. De Goeje.

The same idea is also suggested by further information supplied by the author of the "Contribution" (and which he obtains from *Tabarî*, iii.

1582). It appears that, in the year 865, ten *bârijas* of these people (or of their kindred, the Kerks) ventured up the Tigris from Basra to Baghdad. Each of these "barges" had a complement of forty-five men, composed of the captain; thirty-nine men, of whom some were soldiers and some rowers; three "firemen" (or *grenadiers*, their duty being to attack the enemy with naphtha, or Greek fire); and, lastly, a carpenter and a baker. Thus the total strength of the expedition amounted to four hundred and fifty men.

Whether these bargemen of 865 represented an unsubdued remnant of the Zotts of 834, or whether they were an independent body of Kerks, there is every sign that this nation, or confederacy, possessed a distinct organization—and civilization—of its own. Even the special mention of their *trumpets*, in the sentence describing the entrance into Baghdad of the captive Zottic army, seems to indicate another mark of individuality; for the trumpets are placed side by side with the "national garb." In short, all those traits and customs which the Arab writers think worthy of mention must (inferentially) have been characteristic of the Zott nation, as distinguished from the Arabs.

Some of the offices held by these people when in captivity, may also be noticed here. The 12,000 Zotts sent from India to Persia, in the fifth century, were musicians before anything else; their skill in that art being, indeed, the cause given for their deportation. And we further learn that certain captive Kerks, five centuries later, were employed in the same way, a procession of state prisoners in the streets of Baghdad, in the year 911, being "preceded by the Kork and other musicians." Probably the trumpets borne by the Zott prisoners of 834 only represented one of many varieties of musical instrument in the captive army.

A less dignified office than that of musician remains yet to be noticed. We are told that the subject Zotts in Basra (and also the Sayâbija, a neighbouring, if not a kindred, tribe) were "chiefly employed as policemen and gensdarmes." For these duties, however, it can hardly be said that any special or racial qualifications are necessary. Nevertheless, the statement helps to throw some light upon the uses made of these prisoners by the Arabs; and perhaps something of this kind is meant when it is stated, with regard to the Zotts deported to Ainzarba about the year 835, that "the inhabitants derived much benefit from their services."

NOTE I.—*Mahmûd's Seventeenth Expedition.*

In Elliot's *History of India* (vol. ii. pp. 477, 478) there is an account of this expedition, and the following version is quoted from *Nizámu-d dín Ahmad*:—

"In the same year (417 H.), the Sultán, with a view to punish the Játs, who had molested his army on his return from Somnát, led a large force towards Multán, and when he arrived there he ordered fourteen hundred boats to be built, each of which was armed with three firm iron spikes, projecting one from the prow and two from the sides, so that anything which came in contact with them would infallibly be destroyed. In each boat were twenty archers, with bows and arrows, grenades, and naphtha; and in this way they proceeded to attack the Játs, who, having intelligence of the armament, sent their families into the islands, and prepared themselves for the conflict. They launched, according to some, four, and according to others, eight thousand boats, manned and armed, ready to engage the Muhammadans. Both fleets met, and a desperate conflict ensued. Every boat of the Játs that approached the Moslem fleet, when it received the shock of the projecting spikes, was broken and overturned [while others, it is stated, were set on fire]. Thus, most of the Játs were drowned, and those who were not so destroyed were put to the sword. The Sultán's army proceeded to the places where their families were concealed, and took them all prisoners. The Sultán then returned victorious to Ghaznín."

We are told in Elliot's *History* that this is one of the more problematical of Mahmûd's expeditions, being "recorded only by the later authorities." "But the attack upon the Játs is not in itself improbable, though some of its attendant circumstances are. It is probable that, on the dissolution of the kingdom of Lahore, the Játs of the Júd hills acquired considerable power, and by predatory incursions were able to harry their neighbours. Their advance so far from their own country to attack the Muhammadan army, and the strength of the force with which they opposed it, show that they possessed no inconsiderable power. From a passage quoted by M. Reinaud . . . it appears that they had invaded the principality of Mansúra, and had forced the Musulmán Amír to abjure his religion. It does not quite appear what particular portion of the hilly country is here meant, but most probably the Salt range, on the part nearest to Multán. The Játs have now moved further to the north and east, but some of their clans point to the Salt range as their original seats."

NOTE J.—*The Zotts, Djatts, or Jauts.*

The number of ways in which the name of this people is spelt, and the localities in which they are placed, are very numerous. The name is variously spelt Zott, Zatt, Zath, *Xanthii*, *Xuthi Zuthi*, Zuth, Zûtt, Dyat, Djatt, Jat, Ját (Jāt and Jât), Jath, Juth, Jutt, Jit (*Encyc. Brit.*), *Iatii*, and Jaut. Of these, the italicized forms are problematical, occurring in classical writings, and quoted by General Cunningham. The form *Jaut* (which I have only seen in Lord Combermere's *Memoirs*) appears to offer the best compromise; and its spelling coincides with the popular English form of a similar word *ghât*, viz. *ghaut*.

As regards the districts in which the Jauts are placed by various writers, they include Asia Minor, Syria, Arabia, Persia, Afghanistan, Beluchistan, Northern India, and Central Asia. Dera-Jat, in the Panjâb, is still emphatically "the country of the Jauts."

One account of the Jauts speaks of them as "An Indian people estimated to form two-fifths of the entire population of the Punjab, and half that of the Rájput states. They are also widely spread," continues this writer, "through Sind, Baluchistan, and the North-Western Provinces. Their traditions indicate an immigration from Ghazní, or Kandahar,[1] but writers of authority have identified them with the ancient Getæ, and there is strong reason to believe them a degraded tribe of Rájputs, whose Scythic origin has also been maintained.[2] Dr.

[1] Mr. De Goeje particularly notes that the town of *Gandâra*, *Kandohâr*, or *Kondohâr*, "must not be confounded with the modern Kandahar" (*ante*, pp. 46, 47, note [3]).

[2] "Colonel Tod, still the standard historian of Rájásthán, strongly insisted on this point [the affinity between Rájputs and Jauts]. Some relationship between the Játs and the Rájputs, although obscure, is

Trumpp, however, regards them as the first Aryan settlers in the valley of the Indus, and their language strongly favours this view. . . . In recent times, the valour of the race showed itself in the two sieges of Bhartpur, the seat of a Ját dynasty, in 1805 and 1826, and has long been conspicuous in the military qualities of the Sikhs. They are a migratory stock. . . . They are in general a harmless, industrious people, preserving in songs and legends the memory of better times. Under favourable conditions, however, old predatory habits revive, and their wandering instinct leads them, in the guise of itinerant traders, far into Central Asia. Indeed, there is plausible though not conclusive evidence that the Gipsies owned them as progenitors" (*Encyc. Brit.*, 9th edit., vol. xiii. p. 597). The same account, it may be added, describes them as "extremely dark" in complexion.

Professor Dowson (Elliot's *History of India*, 1869, vol. i. p. 508), remarks: "At the present day the Játs are found in every part of the Panjab, where they form about two-fifths of the population. They are chiefly Musulmáns, and are divided into not less than a hundred different tribes. . . . To the east of the Panjab, the Hindu Játs are found in considerable numbers in the frontier states of

acknowledged; and, although the *jus connubii* no longer exists between them, an inscription shows that they intermarried in the fifth century, A.D." (*Encyc. Brit.*, 9th edit. vol. xii. p. 789).

Bikaner, Jesalmer, and Jodhpur, where, in Colonel Tod's opinion, they are as numerous as all the Rajput races put together.[1] They are found also in great numbers along the upper course of the Ganges and Jumna, as far eastward as Bareli, Farakhabad, and Gwalior, where they are divided into two distinct clans. . . . To the south of the Panjab, the Musulmán Játs are said by Pottinger to fórm the entire population of the fruitful district of Haraud-Dajel, on the right bank of the Indus, and the bulk of the population in the neighbouring district of Kach-Gandava. In Sindh, where they have intermarried largely with Buluchis and Musulmáns of Hindu descent, it is no longer possible to estimate their numbers, although it is certain that a very large proportion of the population must be of Ját descent."

According to Captain Burton (*History of Sindh*, pp. 246, 247: London, 1851), the Jauts constituted, "in the time of the Kalhoras, one of the ruling classes in Sindh. . . . They are supposed to have entered Sindh," he further states, "a little before the accession of the Kalhora princes, and shortly afterwards to have risen to distinction by their superior courage and personal strength. At present they have lost all that distinguished them, and of their multitude of Jagirdars, Zemindars, and Sardars, now not a single descendant possesses anything

[1] See note (2), pp. 78, 79, *ante*.

like wealth or rank. Their principal settlements are in the provinces of Kakralo, Jati, Chediyo, Maniyar, Phulajee, and Johi. They are generally agriculturists or breeders of camels, and appear to be a quiet, inoffensive race of people." We are also told by Captain Burton that, "under the name Jat, no less than four distinct races are comprised;" and, with regard to locality, that "Lieutenant Wood's work shows that the Jats are still found in the Panjab, and all along the banks of the Indus, from its mouth to the Attock."

The identification of these people with gypsies is described by Mr. F. H. Groome (*Encyc. Brit.*, art. "Gipsies"), as "a theory started by Pott, elaborated by Bataillard, and supported by Newbold, Sir H. Rawlinson (*Proceedings of the Geogr. Soc.*, vol. i., 1857), Professor de Goeje (*Bijdrage tot de Geschiedenis der Zigeuners:* Amsterdam, 1875), Captain Burton (*Academy*, March 27, 1875), and a writer in the *Edinburgh Review* (July, 1878)." But he goes on to say, "These writers, however, all agree in making the Gipsies Jats; but none have essayed the necessary comparison of Romani and Játakí (the idiom of the living Indian Jats), though Captain Burton himself has published a grammar of the latter in the *Journal of the Bombay Asiatic Society* (Bombay, 1849)." And he concludes: "In the face of the great unlikeness of Romani and Játakí, one may well concur with Bataillard in the rejection of this theory." In this respect, however, the fact must not be overlooked that language does not form an infallible test of pedigree. There are several gypsy populations by whom the language of the Romané has been forgotten; and everywhere the tendency among gypsies of the present day is to relinquish their ancestral speech. Racial characteristics, before everything else, indicate the lineage of a people; and these ought to be held to corroborate history, or tradition, when they accord with the pedigree thus assigned—and this even in those cases where the *language* of the people in question does not bear a similar testimony.

One more reference to the Jauts may be made here. In writing "On the Gypsies of Bengal," with whom he identifies the tribe of the Bediyás, Dr. Mitra remarks [1] that "when in the neighbourhood of towns or villages, the Bediyá earns his livelihood by thieving, exposing dancing-monkeys, bears, and serpents," etc. And he appropriately adds, "The Luri of Persia and the Multani of Cabul keep bears and monkeys, and all three are attended by wild, half-savage dogs, as are the Bunjáras of central India and the gypsies of Europe.

Now, these "Luri of Persia" are Jauts, and so, apparently, are the "Multani of Cabul." Indeed, the latter would not have been cited along with the Persian Luris and the gypsies of Europe, had

[1] At p. 126 of vol. iii. of the Anthropological Society's *Memoirs*.

the writer not understood them to be gypsies also. Their right to be styled "gypsies" may further be inferred from the fact that Multán (or, at any rate, its neighbourhood) has been associated with the Jauts from time immemorial. So that those of the Jauts whom Reinaud states[1] are found in Cabul at the present day are, no doubt, the "Multani" of Mitra. These, then, with the Persian "Luris" and the European gypsies, figure as leaders of dancing bears and monkeys.

How far the modern Europeans who figure as bear-leaders and monkey-leaders are to be identified with gypsies, is unknown to the present writer. Mr. Bataillard, however, talks of "les Tsiganes conducteurs d'ours, venant la plupart de Bulgarie;"[2] and I notice that, in a woodcut from the *Cosmographie Universelle* of Munster (1552)[3] two of the gypsies therein represented are busied in the background, the one with a *bear*, the other with a boar (though whether they are in conflict with the animals, or are merely putting them through their facings, is a little uncertain). However, it is likely that there are many examples of European gypsies as *ursari*. With regard to monkey-leaders, it is noteworthy (and suggestive, though not proving anything), "that in Turkey at the present day

[1] See *ante*, p. 34.
[2] *Les Gitanos d'Espagne*, p. 35. Lisbon, 1884.
[3] Reproduced in Lacroix's *Manners, etc., of the Middle Ages*.

tchengâne signifies also 'organ-grinder,'" and that possibly the association between the dancing-monkey and the portable organ can be traced back to the Tchengâné themselves. As for the modern gypsies of Egypt, there is no dubiety in this respect, as may be seen from Mr. Leland's statement,[1] made on the authority of the late Captain Newbold: "Many of them are athletes, mountebanks, *and monkey-exhibitors.*"

NOTE K.—*Bhangi.*

In an article "On the Gypsies of Bengal" (*Memoirs of the Anthropological Society of London*, vol. iii.), Dr. Mitra, of Calcutta, states, with regard to the Bediyás, a people whom he compares with the gypsies, that "chiefs of clans assume the title of *bhangy*, or 'drinkers of bhang' (Indian hemp), *par excellence*, as a mark of honour." Mr. De Goeje, on the other hand, applies this title to a whole caste.

It is curious to note that the sect of the *Assassins*, founded by Hasan-ben-Sabbah ("The Old Man of the Mountain") in the eleventh century, was also a caste of *Bhangi*. "It is yet disputed," says the late Mr. Edward Fitzgerald, "whether the word *Assassin*, which they have left in the language of modern Europe as their dark memorial, is derived from the *hashish*, or opiate of hemp-leaves (the

[1] See *The English Gipsies*, p. 198: London, 1874.

Indian *bhang*), with which they maddened themselves to the sullen pitch of oriental desperation, or from the name of the founder of the dynasty." At any rate, whatever be the true etymology, it is evident that they were *hashishim*, or *bhangi*.

NOTE L.—*Jauts and Goths.*

That a gypsy race should be a Gothic race is a belief which, perhaps more than any other of this kind, is at variance with the ideas popularly accepted. Dr. Trumpp, we are told, "has expressed as his opinion, although with some hesitation, that the Jauts are related to the ancient Getæ or Goths." And this opinion is shared by others.

"Writers of authority have identified them [the Jauts] with the ancient Getæ, and there is strong reason to believe them a degraded tribe of Rájputs whose Scythic origin has also been maintained."[1] "Many scholars believe that the Scythians poured down upon India in such masses as to supplant the previous population. The Jits, or Játs, who form nearly one half of the inhabitants of the Punjab, are identified with the Getæ; their great subdivision, the Dhe, with the Dahæ, whom Strabo places on the shores of the Caspian. This view has received the support of most eminent investigators, from Professor H. H. Wilson to General

[1] *Encyc. Brit.*, 9th edit. vol. xiii. p. 597.

Cunningham, the director-general of the archæological survey. The existing division between the Eastern Játs and the Dhe has, indeed, been traced back to the contiguity of the Massa-getæ, or Great Getæ and the Dahæ, who dwelt by the side of each other in Central Asia, and who may have advanced together during the great Scythian movement towards India on the decline of the Bactrian empire. Without pressing such identifications too closely in the service of particular theories, the weight of authority is in favour of a Scythian origin for this most numerous and most industrious section of the population of the Punjab."[1]

The terms "Gothic" and "Scythic" may, of course, prove to be very comprehensive; as comprehensive, for instance, as the term "Asiatic" at the present day. But let us see if there are any minor features of the gypsies which are not inconsistent with a "Gothic" descent.

One such feature we find in the practice which obtained among the gypsies of Galloway up till the close of last century, of staining their faces with ruddle, or hæmatite. This, says Jornandes (or Jordanes), a Goth of the sixth century, was a *Gothic* custom.

Again, the kindred practice of tattooing was also "Gothic." Buchanan, the Scottish historian, draws attention to this. In discussing the possibilities of

[1] *Encyc. Brit.*, vol. xii. p. 789.

the so-called "Picts" of early Britain being of Gothic origin, and while referring to their practice of tattooing, and the likelihood that it indicated a kinship with other tribes following the same practice, he proceeds thus:—"As the Picts, however, marked their skins with iron, and delineated the figures of different animals upon them, it will be, therefore, proper to inquire what nations, either in Scythia, Germany, or the neighbouring countries, were accustomed to paint their bodies, not to inspire terror, but for the purpose of ornament. The Geloni in Thrace, Virgil tells us, were thus accustomed to adorn themselves; and Claudian, speaking of them in his first book against Rusinus, says—

> "'Membraque qui ferro gaudit pinxisse, Gelonus.'

> "'. . . and the Geloni, who delight
> Their hardy limbs with iron to imprint.'

"The same poet mentions the Getæ in Thrace, as ornamenting their bodies in a similar manner:—

> "'Crinigeri sedere patres, pellita Getarum
> Curia, quos plagis decorat numerosa cicatrix.'

> "'The nobles of the long-haired Getæ sat
> In council, skin-clad, and their bodies bore
> The seamy ornament of many a scar.'

"Since then, the Geloni, according to Virgil, were neighbours to the Getæ, and either the Gothuni or Getini, according to Arrian, are numbered among the Getæ, where is the difficulty in supposing that the Picts had originally sprung from among them, especially as Tacitus tells us, the Gothuni spoke Gallic?" (Aikman's Translation of Buchanan's *History of Scotland*, vol. i. pp. 88, 89).[1]

Thus, certain *Gothic* tribes of Europe practised tattooing. Now, we have evidence of *gypsy* tribes who followed the same practice: those of Bengal (*Memoirs of Anthrop. Soc. of London*, vol. iii. p. 127), those of Egypt (Leland's *English Gipsies*, p. 194), those of France (Hoyland, p. 19), and those of England (*In Gipsy Tents*, p. 329), and although this last only refers to an isolated instance, yet that instance suggests others. Accordingly, we have *Gothic* tribes who tattooed themselves, and *gypsy* tribes who practised the same art.

Therefore, since the customs of painting and of tattooing the skin were practised by gypsies and by Goths alike, here is one minor feature which does not disprove the "Gothic" origin of gypsies.

But are we to understand that "Goths" and "gypsies" were alike in *complexion?* When scholars tell us that a certain gypsy race is "one of the ancient Indo-Germanic races of India," "the first Aryan settlers in the valley of the Indus," "identified with the ancient Getæ," do they mean us to infer that those *Getæ*, *Indo-Germans*, and

[1] There is also a copious note relating to the *picti Geloni*, *picti Mauri*, and others, in Ritson's *Annals of the Caledonians, etc.*, pp. 94-96. Edinburgh, 1828.

Aryans, were dark-skinned races? And those tattooed *Geloni* and *Getæ* of the poets, were they also of gypsy hue?[1] So far as the last-named race is concerned, this is not unlikely, if the "Picts" of early Britain were really *Getæ;* because those Picts were compared by Pliny to Ethiopians in complexion, and the poet Claudian calls them "Moors." And certain traders who were wrecked in the Baltic, in the time when L. Metellus Celer was pro-consul of Gaul (*ante*, Note E.), are styled "Indians" by various writers, and are supposed by some to be no other than those "painted Britons," otherwise "Moors" and "Ethiopians." So that, if such British "Picts" were also "Goths," they resembled our Goth-descended Jauts in being of dark complexion, and their custom of tattooing connected them with other gypsy tribes. (For it does not seem to be stated that the Jauts themselves practised tattooing.)

The early Saxons and Danes, also, are understood to have been "Goths," and to have painted and tattooed their skins. Now, these people are spoken of as *nigræ gentes*, *dubh galls*, or *black heathen*, in our early records; and, at a later time, as "Saracens," this last being a common appellation of "Moors" and gypsies. (For which see

[1] It may be noted that a seventeenth-century writer (compiler of *The Cambridge Dictionary*, 1693) says of the Agathyrsi or Geloni that they "are otherwise called Getæ and Tartari," and that "some take them for the Walachians or Moldavians."

Ancient and Modern Britons, vol. i. pp. 113–116, and vol. ii. pp. 438–441: London, 1884.) Here again, then, we have people who were called "Goths" and "Moors," and who also tattooed themselves. The Jauts, therefore, might easily be descended from this kind of "Goths."

Moreover, the Goths themselves are derived from the East, and the Gothic languages are said to be of Indian origin, though they have undergone greater modifications than the gypsy dialects.

The result, therefore, of a few glances at the recognized "Goths" of Europe, is not contradictory of the theory "that the Jauts are related to the ancient Getæ or Goths."

NOTE M.—*Mimus.*

This connection between *Sindi* and *mimus* ("Sindi" being assumed to be "gypsy") has many parallels in Europe.

In speaking of the gypsies of Spain, Mr. De Rochas (*Les Parias de France et d'Espagne*, p. 269: Paris, 1876), says: "Les *Constitutions de Catalogne* les désignent, en 1512, sous les noms de '*Boémians et* sots *nom de boemians*," etc. In Scotland, also, the earlier statutes associate with gypsies "such as make themselves fools," "fancied fools," "professed pleasants," etc. And they are remembered in Holland as mountebanks and jugglers (see De

Goeje), which words denote something closely akin to "buffoon," "*sot*," etc.

NOTE N.—*Rom, Rom'ni, etc.*

Our author remarks that the self-applied name of *Rom* (or *Rom'ni*) is accurate, "because it signifies 'men.'" Moreover, when, in the discussion which followed the reading of Mr. De Goeje's treatise, it was pointed out by a fellow-Academician that gypsies also call themselves *Kalo-Rom*, that term was again translated "black *men*."

Again, it is stated by Dr. Mitra, of Calcutta (in an article "On the Gypsies of Bengal," *Mem. Anthrop. Soc. of London*, vol. iii. p. 121), that "Rominichal" signifies "wandering man;" while a third definition is given by Lacroix (*Manners, etc., during the Middle Ages*, Eng. trans., p. 456: London, 1876), who says that the gypsies of the fifteenth century "called themselves *Romi*, or *gens mariés*."

Thus we have "man," "wanderer," and "husband" variously given as the meaning of the word *rom*. And the writers cited are, in each definition, countenanced by many others.

That *rom* once signified "a man" in a particular language (Coptic, for example), does not seem to be anywhere denied. Borrow, indeed, ascribes to it a still more primitive meaning, out of which the significations "man" and "husband" were afterwards evolved. However that may be, the word *rom* seems to have been used at a very early date to denote "men" or "husbands;"[1] but the men and husbands *of a particular race only.* And this distinction is still drawn. Thus, although *kaulo rom* does really signify "a black man," it is most unlikely that a gypsy would use that expression to describe a black man who was of non-gypsy stock. He would style him *kaulo gairo, kaulo manoosh, kaulo moosh,* or *kaulomengro;* but that a gypsy (an English gypsy, at any rate), in referring to two men not of his race, should speak of one of them as *kaulo rom* ("a black man"), and of the other as *pauno rom* ("a white man"), seems hardly conceivable. For, in England, at least, a *rom* is a *gypsy*-man, before all others.

It is impossible, however, to show that this distinction is everywhere absolutely preserved. For example, when Miklosich gives us some specimens of the language of certain Russian gypsies (those of Ssumy, in the Government of Kharkov), he renders the words "Odová *rom*" by "Hier ist ein *Zigeuner;*" and, in illustrating the declension of nouns, in the same dialect, he gives us *rom* ("Zigeuner"), *barvaló rom* ("reicher Zigeuner"), and *barvalí romní* ("reiche Zigeunerinn"). But,

[1] The terms are often synonymous; *e.g.* in our phrase "man and wife," or among the humbler classes, where "man" is frequently used in the sense of "husband." The twofold use of *weib* in German, and *femme* in French, is a parallel case.

on the other hand, we find in his vocabulary of this dialect that *rom* may either be translated "Mann" or "Zigeuner," and that *romní* is indifferently "Frau" and "Zigeunerinn;" while he also states that *odová manús* (or *manúsh*)—the gypsy for "jener Mensch"—becomes, in the plural, "odolá *romá* oder manusá [or manushá]." Nevertheless, in spite of this twofold application, the general tendency of these extracts (for which see his *Beiträge zur Kenntniss der Zigeunermundarten*, iv. *f.*) is to show that, in this dialect, *rom* is a *gypsy*, rather than any other kind of "man." Indeed, it may be questioned whether those gypsies of Kharkov really meant that *rom*, while signifying "a man," could be fitly applied, or ever was applied by them, to a male *gaujo.*[1]

[1] This word *gaujo*, which signifies "non-gypsy," or "gentile," is the very antithesis of *rom*. Whatever doubt may attach to the application of *rom* (and if there is any, there is very little), it is quite clear that *gaujo*, though signifying "a man," can never, in any conceivable fashion, be applied to a true *gypsy* man.

All the Romané of Europe appear to employ this word to denote the outside world. It has various forms. In England it is *gaújo*, *gaújer*, *górjo*, *gorjer* (Smart and Crofton's *Dialect*), *gorgio* (Borrow and others), *garger* (*English Gipsy Songs*, p. 235); in Scotland it is *gaugie* (Simson's *History*), but at Yetholm *gadgé* (*Ibid.*, p. 334), or *gajo* (Borrow's *Lavo-Lil*, p. 322); while in Ireland it is, according to Simson (*History*, pp. 328, 329), *gaugie*, as in some parts of Scotland. Simson's so-called "gypsies" are, however, far from being pure Romané; and it is no doubt because of this that they apply this term *to themselves*, as well as to other "men." In England (with Wales), which seems at the present day to be the only part of the British Islands that has retained the pure gypsy stock, no *Rom* would ever call himself or another gypsy a *gaujo.*

Rom, having once the signification of "a man," would naturally gain the additional meaning of "a husband;" the former being, indeed, frequently used for the latter, in other languages besides Romanes. But it is manifestly absurd to say that because one of the meanings of *rom* is "husband," therefore the Roms are a race of "*gens mariés*."

In this secondary sense of "husband," the word *rom* seems to be nowadays applied to all "husbands," whether they are Romané or Gaujoes. That is to say, although an English gypsy would not use the words "pauno *rom*" to denote "a white *man*" (who did not happen to be in any sense a gypsy), yet if he were referring to the same man as a "husband," he would employ the word *rom*. In such a sentence as this, "*pauno rom ta kauli romni, dinneleskoe romipen se 'dova*," the supposed husband might be a pure representative of any white race, and his black wife (*kauli romni*) might be a Hottentot. The use of *rom* and *romni* in this manner does not imply, in the least degree,

This last spelling, it may be observed, gives the usual English sound of this word in the masculine gender.

On the Continent the forms are such as these:—In Spain, *gadzo* (De Rochas); in the Basque country, *ogacho*, or *egacho* (Baudrimont and Michel); in the south of Hungary, *gazo;* and in Russia (*e.g.* at St. Petersburg, Moscow, and Ssumy), *gadzo* (Miklosich), or *gajo*, as it is spelt by Mr. C. G. Leland (*The Gypsies*, p. 45). It may be added that these Russian gypsies regard *gadzo* as meaning "peasant," as well as "gentile;" and also that the gypsies of Hungary and Spain have another (and more contemptuous) equivalent of *gaujo*, in the word *busno*.

that the people so indicated are connected with the Rom, or Romané. The words are applied quite impartially to all married people, whether gypsy or gentile.

These remarks hold good on the Continent as well as with us. The late Mr. De Rochas, in his vocabulary of Spanish-Gypsy words, gives *manusch* and *gadzo* (Eng. *manoosh* and *gaujo*) as the general terms for "a man," and *gadzi* (Eng. *gaujï*) as the general term for "a woman;" but of *rom* and (fem.) *romi*, he says: "*Ces noms s'appliquent à l'homme et à la femme de race bohémienne et mariés.*" And, although he subsequently introduces "*Rom*, homme; *romi*, femme; . . . *rom* vel *manusch* . . . *romi* vel *gadzi*" (at pp. 303, 304 of the book referred to—*Les Parias de France et d'Espagne:* Paris, 1876), it must be understood that he had this distinction in mind when he placed these words side by side. Among the Romané of the Hungarian-Carpathian district, the usage is similar. *Rom* is a gypsy man, and *Romńi* a female gypsy; while *romńake*, which stands for "wife" in the accusative case (Miklosich's *Beiträge*, iv. *a.*), is only an inflected form of *romńi.*

Mr. Leland (*The English Gipsies*, 3rd edit. p. 45) makes an English gypsy say that "*rum* is a gipsy, and a *rom* is a husband." Whether this distinction really obtains or not, it is evident that these are only two different pronunciations of one word.

Indeed, it is difficult to decide, sometimes, whether the speaker says "*Rom*many" or "*Rum*many" (when the longer word is used). Borrow recognizes this when he makes Jasper say, "'Tis called *Rommany*," in answer to the remark that his language "must be a *rum* one." And it seems quite clear that our slang adjective *rum* is one of the many slang words that are gypsy, and that it is this same word *rom*, or *rum*. And if Borrow had belonged to an earlier generation, his expression *rum*, as applied to the language of the *Rum*, would not only have been correct, but it would have conveyed nothing derogatory; for we are told that "in Ben Jonson's time, and even so late as Grose," "the word *rum* . . . meant *fine* and *good*." And one writer upon this subject states[1] that "*Rum* still means 'noble and good' among our gypsies," and that *Rum Roy* signifies with them "a gentleman," but (says the same writer, at page 47 of the book quoted from) a *gypsy* gentleman. In short, the "Rum Roy" of the Mitcham gypsies, who are here referred to, is the "Romano Rye" of others. It is enough, however, to point out that *Rom* and *Rum* are merely two pronunciations of one word,[2] without dwelling longer on this detail.

[1] Mr. J. Lucas, at p. 66 of *The Yetholm History of the Gypsies*. Kelso, 1882.

[2] This identity is referred to at pp. 312, 313 of vol. ii. of *Ancient and Modern Britons*. It is also further seen in the fact that a certain wine was known as *Romané*, in Holland, in the year 1562 (see

In the longer forms of the word, by which the gypsies are more generally known, many varieties of accentuation are apparent. Mr. Leland quotes one gypsy who pronounced both "Rommany" and "Rummany" (*English Gipsies*, pp. 40, 44, and 45: 1874); and Mr. Borrow (*Lavo-Lil*, pp. 156, 157) tells us of a Buckinghamshire half-breed who used to say "Roumany." The most usual spelling in (English) books appears to be "Romany." The "Rom'ni" of Mr. De Goeje, or even a quicker sound (as "Rum'ni"), perhaps comes as near the orthodox English pronunciation as any other form.

The popular English usage gives "Romany" as a noun signifying "gypsy;" in the plural, "Romanies." In a "flash" dictionary, published at London in 1827, I find, "*Romoners*—fellows pretending to be acquainted with the occult sciences; fortune-tellers" (a definition which is interesting, in that it shows that the art of divination was quite recently practised by *male* gypsies). But this "Romoner" is evidently only a cockneyfied spelling

Longfellow's *Dutch Language and Poetry*), while in England it was known as *Rumney* (Hazlitt's edition of Dodsley's *Collection*, 1874, vol. i. p. 24). *Romanie* is still the name among the Yetholm gypsies (Simson, p. 333; Lucas, p. 47) for a stronger liquor, known both as *whiskey* and *rum*. In the slang dictionaries, *rum bouse* is a name for "fine drink" of any kind; and in a dictionary of this sort (London, 1827), I find, "*Rum boose*—wine, or any liquor." Thus, whether our modern liquor called "rum" is an abbreviation of the *rumney* of "The Four Elements," above referred to, or whether it comes from the former use of "rum" as an adjective, it is equally derivable from *Rom* and *Romané*.

of the "Romino" (Roberts's *The Gypsies:* London, 1836) and "Romano" of later writers.[1]

The correct forms appear to be *Romano* (masc.), *Romani* (fem.), and *Romané* (plur.). These are not rigidly adhered to even by gypsiologists; and as for the gypsies, they seldom trouble themselves to speak with grammatic correctness a language they are now fast forgetting. Their commonest term for "gypsy" seems to be *Rom'ni-chel* or *Rum'ni-chel* (otherwise, *Rómano-chal*, *Rómani-chal*, etc.); and, in the ordinary broken speech, the plural is formed by adding *s*—among English gypsies, that is to say. The correct plural of *chal* or *chel* (which means "lad" or "fellow"), is formed by adding *é* or *aw*.[2] Although so frequently used, "Roman*i*-chal" is incorrect, as the terminal *i* indicates the feminine. "Roman*o*-chal" is thus preferable, and this form is occasionally met with.

These remarks refer chiefly to England, but they also apply, in some degree, to the continental gypsies. "Rom" is used to denote one of themselves by the gypsies of Spain, of the Hungarian Carpathians, of Southern Hungary, and of Russia (Kharkov). These are only a few instances;[3] but

[1] This latter spelling occurs, for example, in Borrow's *Lavo-Lil* (p. 138), and in Groome's *In Gipsy Tents* (p. 46).

[2] These statements are gathered from the works of Messrs. Borrow, Crofton, Smart, and Groome. "Romani-chal" seems the most frequent spelling, although a somewhat limited experience would incline the present writer to prefer "Rum'ni-chel."

[3] Taken from Miklosich's *Beiträge*, iv. (*a*), (*b*), and (*f*); and from De Rochas' *Les Parias, etc.*, p. 294.

there is no reason to doubt the truth of Mr. Leland's dictum, that "Rom" is used by gypsies "all the rest of the world over." And the more extended form, usually spelt "Romani-chal" by English writers, seems to be as well known. One sees it referred to as "Rómano-chal" in Germany,[1] and as "Romanichal" in Russia.[2] In the neighbourhood of the Pyrenees, specially in the Basque districts of France, the gypsy calls himself *Romanichel*, *Romanicel*, *Roumancel*, or *Rama-itçéla*. These are the various spellings[3] given by Michel, Baudrimont, and De Rochas.[4] The last-named writer gives the

[1] *In Gipsy Tents*, p. 45.

[2] *The Gypsies*, C. G. Leland, 1882, p. 32.

[3] In every case, these are not the *precise* spellings, for the two last examples are frequently written "Erroumancel" and "Errama-itçéla." But Mr. Baudrimont justly observes: "*Errama* ou *Errouman* doivent être réduits immédiatement à *Rama* et *Rouman*, en supprimant la particule *er*, qui vient très probablement du basque, et précède toujours la lettre *r*." It is obvious that this particle *er* ought to be discounted; but it may be questioned whether it is really an addition from the *Basque* language. We see the same peculiarity in the Spanish-Gypsy *erajai* and *erucal* (Eng. Gyp., *rashi* and *rook*), as well as in the instances just given, and in the Basque-Gypsy *ogacho* or *egacho* (Span. Gyp., *gadzo*; Eng. Gyp., *gaujo*). It also appears in the Hungarian-Gypsy *eray*, which is represented elsewhere by *rai*, or *rye* (this Hungarian example being found in Borrow's *Romany Rye*, 3rd edit, pp. 147, 148). And also among the words given in Samuel Roberts's *Gypsies* (London, 1836); *e.g. acola*, *alullo*, *apono*, *arai*, *araunah*, and *arincina*, for *kaulo*, *lullo*, *pauno*, *rai*, *raunie*, and *rinkeni*. One is tempted to suggest that this prefix may be the Arabic *al*, or *el*—the *l* of which disappears before other consonants. Whether this is an explanation that might be substantiated or not, it seems clear that the peculiarity here spoken of is not confined to the Basque provinces.

[4] See *Le Pays Basque*, F. Michel, p. 144, Paris, 1857; Baudri-

preference to *Romanichel*, although he had frequently heard the pronunciation *Romanicel*. He does not seem to have met with the *Roumancel* (*er-Roumancel*), and *Rama itçéla* (*er-Rama-itçéla*) of Michel and Baudrimont. As for the Italian gypsies, a non-acquaintance with the writings of Ascoli, or of any other than Borrow, upon this division of the subject, compels me to be contented with what is stated in *The Zincali* (4th edit. p. 249), that the Romané of Italy speak "a dialect very similar" to that of their kindred in Spain; whence one may infer that they too style themselves "Romanichals," "Rom," and "Romané." The Italian dance, called the *romanesca* suggests by its name a kinship with the dance of the Spanish *gitanos*, called the *romalis*, of which Mr. Augustus J. C. Hare speaks in his *Wanderings in Spain*.

Besides *Rom*, *Romano*, and *Romano-chal* (or *Rum'ni-chal*), there is the term *Romano-chavo*,[1] used by the gypsies of the Hungarian Carpathians and of Moscow (according to Miklosich's *Beiträge*, iv. pp. 8 and 24). It may be added that in Hungary, the accent in "Romano" is laid on the *second*

mont's *Vocabulaire de la langue des Bohémiens, etc.*, p. 22, Bordeaux, 1862; and *Les Parias de France et d'Espagne*, by V. De Rochas, p. 265, Paris, 1876.

[1] This word *chavo* (sometimes *chabo*) has the same meaning as *chal;* and as Borrow, rightly or wrongly, derives *chal* from the same root as the Scotch *chiel*, so may *chabo*, or *chavo*, be connected with *chap*. All of these words, at any rate, are synonymous, whatever their etymology.

syllable, an instance of which is seen in *In Gipsy Tents* (p. 40).

The language itself is called "Romany" in English "cant," as well as in ordinary English, and in French; but with the Romané themselves it is *Romanes, Rommanis, Romanís, Romanish,*[1] *Rummanis,* and *Rom'nimus.* I am informed that *Róm'nimus* (as used at p. 135 of *In Gipsy Tents*) is the most to be preferred of all. *Romano Jib* (tongue) is also used. The adverb is *Romaneskaes,* or *Romaneskoenæs* (Leland and Borrow).

The pronunciation of Thomas Herne, a semi-gypsy of Buckinghamshire, is thus referred to by Borrow (*Lavo-Lil,* p. 157):—"Instead of saying Romany, like other gypsies, he said Roumany, a word which instantly brought to my mind Roumain, the genuine, ancient name of the Wallachian tongue and people." And, indeed, Borrow makes no distinction between "Roumainesk" (Roumanean) and "Romaneskoenæs" (after the gypsy fashion). Baudrimont also expresses a like opinion, in referring to the same accentuation among the gypsies of the Basque provinces. And as "Roumania" and "Roumelia" are names derived from the race of "the Roum" (otherwise spoken of as "the Byzantines"), one might be disposed to assume

[1] This exceptional form is supplied by Mr. J. Lucas (*The Yetholm History of the Gypsies,* p. 140, where also *Romanís* is given). Mr. Leland uses *Rummanis* in his *English Gipsies* (3rd edit. p. 45).

that the Zotts who were brought into the Byzantine Empire in the year 855 had, in course of time, identified themselves with this nationality, and assumed its name. But, before this solution could be accepted, it would be necessary to first answer satisfactorily the questions—"Why is the name of *Rom* or *Rum* so peculiarly associated with gypsy races?" and "What kind of people, ethnologically regarded, were these same 'Roum' who took captive the Zotts, and who were already known as 'the Roum?'" This would ultimately lead us to question the origin of the name "Roman," whether applied to modern gypsies or to still earlier "Romans." Borrow undoubtedly regards a connection between these two "Roman" races as possible, and even probable. He also very frequently translates the gypsy "Romano" into English "Roman;" and, at p. 47 of *In Gipsy Tents*, there is an instance of an English gypsy (Lucretia Boswell) who regarded the gypsy word *Romani* as equivalent to "a Roman woman."

Mr. De Goeje's impression that the name *Rom* is unknown among Eastern gypsies, appears, from a statement of Mr. C. G. Leland's, to be erroneous. We are informed by the latter writer[1] that there exists in India a caste of genuine gypsies, recog-

[1] *The Gypsies*, 1882, p. 336, *et seq.* Mr. Leland also states, on the authority of the late Captain Newbold, F.R.S., that one division of the gypsies of modern Egypt bears the name of "Romani" (see *The English Gipsies*, 3rd edit. p. 198).

nized as such before all others, who style themselves and their language *Rom.* This information he obtained from a Hindu who had, when young, lived with these people, and his informant was very positive in the matter (whether he was entitled to be so or not). "These people were, he declared, 'the *real* gypsies of India, and just like the gypsies here.'" They "called themselves and their language *Rom.* Rom meant in India a real gypsy. And Rom was the general slang of the road." As in this country, there are in India various nomadic castes; but "among all these wanderers there is a current slang of the roads, as in England. This slang extends even into Persia. Each tribe has its own, but the name for the generally spoken *lingua franca* is *Rom.*" One example given by this man was *manro,* "bread;" which, remarks Mr. Leland, "is all over Europe the gypsy word for bread."

This Hindu further stated, with regard to those Eastern *Roms,* that "people in India called them Trablūs, which means Syrians, but they were full-blood Hindus, and not Syrians."

In naming some of those districts in which the compound word *Romano-chavo* seems to be used instead of *Romano-chal,* I ought to have included Alsace. Mr. Bataillard, referring to *chavo* (everywhere a gypsy word for "boy" or "lad"), says, "Sometimes the gypsies employ this word as a race-name, usually in conjunction with the adjective

Romano. Thus, the Alsatian gypsies often say *Romané chavé* (gypsy lads), in place of simple *Roma.*" (Proceedings of the Ninth Session of the *Congrès international d'anthropologie et d'archéologie préhistoriques*, in 1880, p. 511; or page 29 of Mr. Bataillard's article itself, extracted from the Proceedings, and named *Les Gitanos d'Espagne et les Ciganos de Portugal:* Lisbon, 1884.)

Further, as I had not examined Dr. Paspati's valuable work[1] at the time of writing the main portion of this Note, his remarks upon this subject, which I have since read, are so instructive that, although they will considerably lengthen out an already long enough series of references, it seems desirable to make the following quotations:—

"One thing of great interest in the history of this people is the name *Rom*, by which they name themselves, wherever they are found, whether in Turkey or in the most remote parts of Europe. All the other names given to them are of alien origin, and they avoid the term Tchinghiané, which is an opprobrious designation" (p. 19). "This term *Rom*, when used by gypsies, either of the Sedentary or of the Nomadic class, has three very distinct meanings: (1) *a gypsy*, (2) *a man* (any man), (3) *a husband.* In listening to their tales and songs, it is often very difficult to know when the term *rom*

[1] *Études sur les Tchinghianés ou Bohémiens de l'empire ottoman.* Constantinople, 1870.

is meant to signify a man of their own race, and when it is used to denote any man. *Manúsh*, 'a man,' so frequently used by the Sedentary class, is rare among the Nomads, who generally apply the word *gadjó* to all men of non-gypsy stock. In the few tales still surviving among the wild Zapáris,[1] whose degraded condition has deprived them of the taste for those nocturnal amusements which their Sedentary and most of their Nomadic brethren run after, every man is called a *rom*. In their conversation, on the other hand, they never err; they apply the term *rom* to the men of their race, just as Musulmans give the name of *Islam* to all those who profess the faith of the Prophet. But, in spite of themselves, the poverty of their language often obliges them to extend the designation of *rom* to strangers.[2] Nevertheless, the primitive signification of the word is retained with a remarkable tenacity" (p. 462). One portion of them, those whose winter residence is at Tokát, in Asia Minor (province of Sivas), pronounce their name as *Lom*: but this, Dr. Paspati points out, is only a more liquid sound of the letter *r*, which interchange, he shows us, is also witnessed among the gypsies of the Basque provinces.[3] *Romále* also occurs, as the vocative singular form, in a song of

[1] The least civilized division of the Turkish gypsies.

[2] This slightly qualifies the statement immediately preceding.

[3] For this he refers to Ascoli's *Zigeunerisches*, p. 155. (See *Paspati*, pp. 17 and 340.)

the Nomads. These are slight differences; but, in speaking of some of the gypsies of Asia Minor (where the race is "very numerous"), Dr. Paspati says, "Their language does not differ essentially from that of the Nomads of Roumelia" (p. 16). One form which they occasionally use among themselves indicates a contempt for their own race. This is *Romaní* or *Romni tchik*, equivalent to "gypsy slut." But as this expression is more the property of the *Sedentary* class, whose blood is not pure gypsy, it is likely that the term did not come into use until a mongrel race had arisen, whose sympathies were chiefly with their non-gypsy kindred.[1] The word *Romazán* has a kindred meaning, and is probably of like origin.

As among the other branches of the Romané, *romní*,[2] among the Turkish gypsies, signifies "a wife;" being, as Dr. Paspati points out, the abbreviated feminine form of *romanó*, viz. *rom(a)ní*.[3] A diminutive of this, *romnorí*, seems also common.

[1] Compare also *Simson*, p. 195, note. A parallel case is that of the American mulatto (or even negro) who will call another negro "a low nigger;" the term, and the mental attitude, being derived from the whites.

[2] "I have heard *romní* pronounced *gomní*" (p. 463). Probably this initial *g* ought only to be regarded as a more guttural enunciation of *r*; for these two letters, when pronounced in the guttural fashion, are practically one.

[3] The inflected form *romnidke* occurs among the Nomads; which may be compared with the *romñake* of the Hungarian-Carpathian gypsies (Miklosich's *Beiträge*, iv. *a*). The former is used in the dative singular, the latter in the accusative; but in both cases it is evident that the nominative form is *romní*.

Dr. Paspati further states that *Romanó* is used as an adjective, the language being known as *Romaní tchip* (elsewhere *tschib*, *tchib*, or *jib*). *Romanés* is defined to be an adverb; which bears out the statement of one of our English gypsiologists that, while to *rokker Romanes* means "to speak gypsy," yet the proper term for the language itself (in England, at least) is *Rómˈnimus*.

These researches of Dr. Paspati's, extending as they do from the European parts of Turkey as far eastward as the banks of the Euphrates,[1] show very clearly that the gypsies of the Ottoman Empire, like those of Europe, are *Romané*. That is to say, that a certain widely-scattered family, speaking substantially one language, applies everywhere the term *Rom* (in one shape or another) to its members; although known to "*gaujoes*" by an almost innumerable variety of names. According to Mr. C. G. Leland, the people thus described are found as far south as modern Egypt, and as far east as India; while Miklosich shows them to us in Siberia. As for the etymology of *Rom*, Dr. Paspati suggests its connection with the Sanskrit *Rãma*, and its cognates; and compares with it the Latin *Roma*, *Romanus*, and *Romana*.[2]

The antipodes of *Rom*, viz. *gaujo*, must also be again referred to, in connection with the Turkish gypsies. Among them the pronunciation is *gadjó*

[1] Page 16, l. 29. [2] Page 19-21.

(fem. *gadjí*); and the word is used in much the same fashion as in Europe. For the Turkish gypsy, as for his brethren elsewhere, *gadjó* denotes "every one who is not of his race: Christian, Jew, or Musulman. . . . This is invariable. In his songs and stories, the gypsy never speaks of one of his race as a *gadjó*." A saying of theirs, *Rom romésa, gadjó gadjésa* (gypsy with gypsy, gentile with gentile) represents the antagonism of the words and of the types. The Turkish gypsies, however, apply *gadjó* in a sense apparently rare in western Europe. We are told that "Like *Rom*, it has often the meaning of 'husband' (*gadjí* signifying, equally, 'wife'), especially[1] when the story recounts the deeds of foreigners." "The fact that *gadjó* is used by the Asiatic gypsies leads me to believe that the word is of Indian origin." (See pp. 3, 23, 235, and 236.)

It may be added that *kutúr* is equivalent to *gadjó* among the Asiatic gypsies (p. 301), and that the Musulmans are known by the name of *khorakhái* (akin to the Spanish words *corajai* and *corajano*).

[1] Here, again, the element of uncertainty is introduced. For it seems one has to infer that the word *is* used, if only occasionally, to denote a *gypsy* husband. (Compare *Simson*, p. 326.)

NOTE O.—*The Egyptians or Gitanos.*

It would be superfluous to adduce any proofs in support of our author's assertion that "beyond a doubt" the name *Gitano* is only a form of *Egyptian*, if it were not that the mistake he points out has been made by more than one learned writer. Not that, so far as I am aware, there has been any other instance in which *Gitano* has been assumed to signify *Jatano*. But it has not always been realized that *Gitano* is simply a corruption of *Egiptiano*; just as our *gypsy* is a corruption of *Egyptian*. For example, in writing about *The Gypsies of Bengal*, Dr. Mitra refers to "the Spanish name *gitana*, which was used to indicate the crafty character of the people." Now, although *gitána* does mean "a flatterer," and although other words derived from it, such as *gitanáda*, *gitanaménte*, and *gitaneár*, all denote this quality of "flattery" or "blandishment," it is quite evident that these words have come from *gitána* (in the masc. *gitáno*) in its earliest sense of *Egyptian*; owing to these well-known characteristics of the gypsy people. These terms may of course be applied nowadays to "flatterers" of any race; and in English we have something similar in our uses of the word "gypsy" (*e.g.* "a little gypsy," "gypsy-like," etc.—expressions which may be applied to many who are not gypsies).

The late Mr. De Rochas, in speaking of the

gitanos, says: "Ce nom n'est qu'une contraction d'*Egiptianos* sous lequel ils furent d'abord désignés en Castille." And Mr. Bataillard, similarly, remarks that this name "*Gitanos*, primitivement *Egypcianos*, est le même que celui d'*Égyptien*, l'un des premiers qui eurent cours en France, et que celui de *Gipsies* qui est leur principal nom en Angleterre." Its connection with the last-named form is still more evident in the spelling *Egipcios*, which is quoted in the same treatise.[1] These earlier Spanish forms differ very slightly from our own; *e.g.* *Egiptians* (1510), *Egipcians* (1520), *Gypsions* (1513 and 1524), *Gipcy* (1526), *Gipcyans* (1536), *Egipcyans*, or *Egipsyans* (1537), *Egiptians* (1549) *Giptian* (1578), *Gyptian* and *Gipsen* (1591), *Gipsy* (1593), and *Egipcyans*, or *Egipcians* (1596).[2] There can be no doubt that these English names only differ in the most trifling details from one another, and from those of Spain. And it is equally evident that they relate to the same kind of people. The only difference between the modern Spanish and English names is, that, by the accidents that guide nomenclature, the Spaniards have chosen the form *Egiptiano*, which they have shortened to *'gi't'ano*, while we have altered *Egipsyan* to *'Gipsy'*.

It may be added that the Catalonian pronunciation of *gitáno* differs from that of the rest of Spain.

[1] *Les Gitanos d'Espagne et les Ciganos de Portugal.* Lisbon, 1884.

[2] These spellings will all be found in Mr. Crofton's *English Gipsies under the Tudors.* Manchester, 1880.

Mr. De Rochas informs us that in Roussillon, in the south of France, this word is pronounced *à la façon catalane et française.* But, as he explains that Roussillon was formerly a part of Catalonia, and that the gypsies of Roussillon are the "brothers" of those of Catalonia, it is to be presumed that the Roussillon gypsies are styled "*gitanos*" for these reasons, and that the pronunciation referred to is distinctive of Catalonia rather than of France. Probably, it is the existence of this special pronunciation that has caused one Spanish writer to spell the name with a *j*—thus, *Jitanos.*[1]

Mr. Bataillard states that one of the first names given in France to the gypsies was that of *Égyptien*; and one may see this illustrated in the legend attached by Callot to one of his famous sketches of gypsies, of whom he says, "*qu'ils sont venus d'Aegipte.*" (And these same engravings are catalogued as "4 planches des *Egyptiens,*" in the year 1691.) Thus, we see that in Spain, France, England, and Scotland, these people were once known as "Egyptians." To this list of countries I can also (on the authority of Professor De Goeje) add Holland; although there they seem to be nowadays only spoken of as *Heidens* and *Zigeuners.* With the Dutch, as with the French, the name of *Egyptian* is no longer in vogue. Conversely, the name of *Bohemian,* which was once as well known

[1] See a reference to his book in Bataillard's *Les Gitanos.*

in the Peninsula as *Egyptian*, has died out of the Spanish vocabulary, while it is almost the exclusive term employed in France (for *Tsigane* does not seem to be a popular term, and *Égyptien* is rarely used). But if we were to consider the various and numerous designations given to the "Egyptians" of Europe, we should be led far away from the subject of the above remarks.

The present English spelling, it may be noticed, is indifferently "gipsy" and "gypsy." Each is correct, and each has plenty of precedents. If it were necessary to decide upon so trifling a matter, the preference might be given to "gypsy," on the ground that we no longer spell Egypt and Egyptian with an *i;* although both "Egipt" and "Egiptian" were frequently used at one time.

NOTE P.—*Gypsies as Musicians.*

Whether it be right or not to regard *Zigeuner*, *Zigán*, etc., as signifying "musician," it must be agreed that this translation would be peculiarly appropriate. When the *Turkish* form of the name is considered, there seems, indeed, no doubt that "musician" and "gypsy" are synonyms. And the special branch of the gypsy stem which is treated of in the foregoing "Contribution" is first represented to us by "12,000 musicians of both sexes," who were transported from India to Persia in the fifth century of our era. These people were styled, alternatively, *Lûris* and *Jauts*, and in Syria they were sometimes called *Motribîya*, which also signifies "musicians." We are told that they were "players upon stringed instruments and drums;" although it is not to be supposed that their musical powers were not exercised upon other instruments than these. The special mention of *trumpets*, as one of the distinguishing peculiarities of those conquered Jauts who were brought up the Tigris into Baghdad in the year 834, suggests that this musical instrument was identified with that race. About eighty years after this event, we again hear of the Jauts as musicians. "It is noteworthy," remarks Professor De Goeje, "that the Kork figure as musicians at Bagdad in the year 911. Arîb (manuscr. of Gotha, f. 472) describes a procession of state prisoners in the streets of the metropolis 'preceded by the Kork and other musicians.'" And if the Kork, or Kerks, were not always identical with the Jauts, they were at any rate their near kinsmen.

That "gypsies have always been famous for their musical talents," is a statement not likely to be contradicted; and it applies to Europe as well as to Asia. But while the influence of the gypsies on the music of Europe is recognized, it may be questioned whether it is sufficiently realized. That gypsies have been nomadic musicians in Europe, during several centuries, is admitted by all. But is it only a matter of a few centuries? One title that used to be given to these people, and that is still applicable to them (in a restricted sense), is sufficient of itself to suggest that gypsy minstrelsy in Europe is an affair of more than modern, or comparatively modern, date. This is the name of *juggler*.

It is well known that gypsies are, or were, recognizable as (*saltimbanques*, or *goochelaars*, or jugglers in the various states of Europe. In our own country, and perhaps in others, this is scarcely perceptible at the present day. But Blackstone, in his *Commentaries*, defines gypsies as "a strange kind of commonwealth among themselves of wandering impostors and *jugglers*." Samuel Rid, in his *Art of Juggling* (1612), says that many of them are "juglers." Spenser, in 1591, talks of "a gipsen or a juggeler." And such expressions as these: "The counterfeit Ægyptians . . . practising the art called *sortilegium*. . . . The Ægyptians' juggling witchcraft or sortilegie standeth much in fast or loose," occur in Reginald Scot's *Discovery of Witchcraft*, published in 1584.[1] In a Scottish enactment of the year 1579, "the idle people calling themselves Egyptians" are classed under the same

[1] These quotations are taken at second hand from Mr. Crofton's *English Gipsies under the Tudors*. I also remember to have seen "a band of jugglers or gypsies" incidentally mentioned, but I am unable to give the reference.

denomination as "all idle persons going about in any country of this realm, using subtle crafty and unlawful plays, as jugglery, fast and loose, and such others." These are some instances out of many, in which gypsies appear as *jugglers.*

"The true art of *Juglers* consisteth in legerdemain," says Samuel Rid, writing in 1612. And the word "juggler" has now come to bear this meaning exclusively, in English. But at one time it had a much more extensive application. We are told by a writer of the thirteenth century[1] "that the *Joglar* sings and dances, plays instruments, or enchants people, or does other *joglayria.*" In short, the *juggler* was a musician also; and this part of his profession is better remembered in connection with another pronunciation of the same word, viz. *jongleur.*

That *Jongleurs* and *Jugglers* were one and the same has been clearly shown by various writers. It is enough, for the present purpose, to quote the following from Sismondi; who himself quotes the instructions of a *jongleur* of Gascony, regarding the duties of one of his brotherhood. "He tells him that he must know how to compose and rhyme well, and how to propose a *jeu parti.* He must play on the tambourine and the cymbals, and make the symphony resound. To throw and catch little

[1] De Bezers, whom (as well as Samuel Rid) I quote here from Mr. Lucas's *Yetholm History of the Gypsies*, pp. 86–88.

balls on the point of a knife; to imitate the song of birds; to play tricks with the baskets; to exhibit attacks of castles,[1] and leaps (no doubt, of monkeys)[2] through four hoops; to play on the citole and the mandore; to handle the claricord and the guitar; to string the wheel with seventeen chords, to play on the harp, and to adapt a gigue so as to enliven the psaltry, are indispensable accomplishments. The Jongleur must prepare nine instruments with ten chords, which, if he learns to play well, will be sufficient for his purpose; and he must know how to sound the lyre and the bells." We are also informed by Sismondi that "The Jongleurs (*Joculatores*) used to take their stations in the cross-roads, clothed in grotesque habits, and attract a crowd around them, by exhibiting dancing apes, legerdemain tricks, and the most ridiculous antics and grimaces. In this manner they prepared their audience for the verses which they recited; and they cared not what extravagancies they committed, provided they were well rewarded." And reference is also made to the Charlatans, a division of the *Jongleurs*, "who amused the people by their buffooneries, exhibiting dancing apes and goats, and singing the grossest songs in public."[3]

[1] ? Dramatic representation, or panorama.

[2] This interpolated remark is Sismondi's.

[3] These extracts are from Sismondi's *Historical View of the Literature of the South of Europe*, Roscoe's Translation, 2nd edit. vol. i. pp. 127, 128, 144, 145, 147, and 148. London, 1846.

This, then, was *joglayria*, or jugglery, the profession of the *jongleur*, or juggler. But nowhere in the accounts I have cited, or in any other description of those early[1] jugglers, which I have seen, is there any reference to the *complexion* of the jugglers; with one exception. This special and exceptional instance is furnished by Sir Walter Scott; and although I have made use of it elsewhere, I again refer to it, because it seems to convey a distinct truth. Scott, then, quotes the following "instance in romance," in one of his notes to *Ivanhoe* (Note B.): "John of Rampayne, an excellent juggler and minstrel, undertook to effect the escape of Audulf de Bracy, by presenting himself in disguise at the court of the King, where he was confined. For this purpose, 'he stained his hair and his whole body entirely as black as jet, so that nothing was white but his teeth,' and succeeded in imposing himself on the King, as an Ethiopian minstrel. He effected, by stratagem, the escape of the prisoner." And from this story Scott is led to believe that black men were known in England during the days of "romance." And he could not well have arrived at any other conclusion.

What Scott, however, failed to reflect upon was that these black men were *jongleurs*. Now, *jongleurs* were "of both sexes," like Behram Gour's imported musicians; as one can see from such a passage as

[1] I am here speaking of the jugglers of the Middle Ages.

this: "William de Girmont, Provost of Paris, 1331, prohibited the *Jungleurs* and *Jungleuresses* from going to those who required their performances in greater numbers than had been stipulated. In 1395 their libertinism again incurred the censure of the Government."[1] If these female jugglers, therefore, were of the same complexion as the male jugglers simulated by John of Rampayne, we should have in these wandering mountebanks and musicians of the fourteenth century, a caste of people closely resembling, if not identical with, gypsies.

Indeed, what has just been written about them very nearly amounts to saying that a portion (at any rate) of the early *jugglers* were simply *gypsies.* Sismondi's descriptions of jugglers are almost word for word the same as the accounts given of gypsies. The *professional* caste is pictured as consisting of dancers and musicians, mountebanks, ballad-singers, and buffoons, who "used to take their stations in the cross-roads, clothed in grotesque habits, and attract a crowd around them, by exhibiting dancing apes, legerdemain tricks, and the most ridiculous antics and grimaces." The *gypsy* caste is described in exactly similar words. Professor De Goeje[2]

[1] From Dr. Burney's *History of Music*, here quoted from Mr. Lucas's *Yetholm Gypsies.* The *Yetholm Gypsies* (which contains many interesting and valuable statements) gives considerable information regarding "jugglers" at pp. 85–91.

[2] In a tract entitled *De Heidens of Zigeuners*, extracted from No. 8 of the publication *Eigen Haard*, 1876.

states that the gypsies of Western Europe are, before anything else, mountebanks and ballad-singers. And the Scotch statutes against "Egyptians," from the time of James II. (the fifteenth century) onward, class these people with "vagabonds, bards, juglers, and such like," bards "pretending liberty to bard and flatter," "fancied fools" or "professed pleasants," "all idle persons going about in any country of this realm, using subtle crafty and unlawful plays, as jugglery, fast and loose, and such others; . . . and all minstrels, songsters, and tale-tellers" (with certain reservations regarding these last). The English statutes, already partly referred to, are in similar terms (though perhaps not so copious in expression). And we have seen (*ante*, Note M.) that in Catalonia, in the year 1512, laws were passed against "gypsies, and *fools* styled gypsies;" while, in the East, *mimus* and *sindi* (*i.e.* gypsy) were once interchangeable terms. Finally, we have already seen evidences that both in the East and the West, the exhibition of dancing and performing apes has been associated with gypsy people.[1]

[1] The connection between gypsies and "jugglery" is also referred to, in terms similar to the above, in *Ancient and Modern Britons*, vol. i. pp. 137, 138, 139, 142, 143, 145, 296, and 297, and vol. ii. pp. 316–321.

Lacroix also describes those mediæval jugglers as exhibitors of performing bears; with which may be compared the remarks in the latter part of Note J., *ante* (see Lacroix's *Manners, etc., during the Middle Ages*, pp. 224, 225. London, 1876).

"In the sixteenth century these dancers and tumblers became so numerous that they were to be met with everywhere, in the provinces as well as in the towns. Many of them were Bohemians or Zingari. They travelled in companies, sometimes on foot, sometimes on horseback, and sometimes with some sort of a conveyance containing the accessories of their craft and a travelling theatre."[1] But the sixteenth century is too near our own time for the present question. On what authority Kingsley styles one of the reputed authors of the Nibelungen-Lied "a *Zingar* wizard," I do not know; but it seems that this man (*Klingsohr*, *Cling Zor*, or *Clyncsor*) lived in that part of Hungary known as "The Seven Castles,"[2] and was a celebrated fortune-teller, necromancer, and astrologer.[3] On this showing, then, a gypsy jongleur of the thirteenth century was the possible author of the Nibelungen-Lied.

And this, of course, means that one, at least, among the Hungarian jugglers of the thirteenth century was a gypsy; which brings us back to the

[1] Lacroix, *op. cit.*, p. 230. Compare also *Ancient and Modern Britons*, vol. i. pp. 350, 399, and 400, and vol. ii. p. 329, in connection with this reference to a travelling theatre. And also the quotation from Sismondi bearing upon the exhibition of "attacks of castles," as a part of the juggler's profession.

[2] Which, if it be the district called *Zevenbergen* by the Dutch, and *Siebenbergen* by the Germans, is our *Transylvania*.

[3] He is referred to in *The Saint's Tragedy* (in the text, and in one of the "Notes to Act V."), and Kingsley quotes the particulars regarding him from Dietrich the Thuringian.

era in question—the time of the wandering mountebanks, dancers, and musicians, known as *Jugglers* or *Jongleurs.*

Thus, by regarding the gypsies as musicians, we reach the hypothesis that they have "been famous for their musical talents" throughout Europe, not only during the past few centuries. but as far back as the Middle Ages.

Nor is it necessary to draw the line at that period. The statutes enacted against "jungleurs" and "jungleuresses" in the fourteenth century seem clearly to hint that those people constituted a distinct *caste;* that is, that they were united by the bonds of kinship, as well as by those of kindred habits. And Lacroix tells us that they had their own "kings;" regarding whom he says: "These kings of jugglers exercised a supreme authority over the art of jugglery and over all the members of this jovial fraternity. It must not be imagined that these jugglers merely recited snatches from tales and fables in rhyme; this was the least of their talents. The cleverest of them played all sorts of musical instruments, sung songs, and repeated by heart a multitude of stories,[1] after the

[1] 'One of the most marked characteristics of the Gaelic *seanachaidh*, who belonged to the bardic order in Ireland and Scotland. Walker, in his *Memoirs of the Irish Bards*, states that one division of the bards was composed of "Panegyrists or Rhapsodists, in whom the characters of the Troubadour and Jongleur of Provence seem to have been united." The Irish Rhapsodists he is here speaking of were of the eleventh century.

example of their reputed forefather, King Borgabed, or Bédabie, who, according to these troubadours, was King of Great Britain at the time that Alexander the Great was King of Macedonia."[1] From this, therefore, it appears that the fourteenth-century jugglers of France possessed laws and leaders of their own, and that they also regarded themselves as a distinct people, possessed of a national history.

Whether the *jongleurs* of Ireland, in the eleventh century (referred to in the *Memoirs of the Irish Bards*), also believed themselves to be descended from a British monarch of the fourth century B.C., is apparently not stated. But those of France identified themselves (see Lacroix, p. 225) with that juggler of the eleventh century who distinguished himself at the battle of Hastings. And it is to be inferred from Lacroix's statements that he (though in his own person an alien invader) was descended, or believed himself to be descended, from a caste of jugglers whose presence in the British Islands dated as far back as the fourth century B.C.

But the point to be attended to is the complexion of these jugglers of the eleventh century and afterwards. According to the *Ivanhoe* "instance in romance," many of them were "Ethiopian minstrels." Now, although this traditional story

[1] Lacroix's *Manners, etc., of the Middle Ages*, pp. 123, 124: London, 1876.

was taken as an isolated statement, it is only isolated so far as regards the jugglers *of the Middle Ages.* One finds "Ethiopian" minstrels and jugglers in England at a period preceding the John-of-Rampayne story by something like a thousand years. When, in the beginning of the third century A.D., the Emperor Severus was in Britain, we are told that as he was returning to one of his stations there, "not only victor, but also, a peace being established for ever, revolving in his mind everything that might happen to him, a certain Æthiop out of the military number, of great fame among the minstrels, and always of celebrated jokes, met him with a crown made of cypress; whom when he, being angry, had commanded to be removed from his sight, smitten by the omen as well of his complexion as of the crown, he is said to have uttered, by way of joke, 'Thou hast been all things, hast conquered all things, now, victor, be a god.'"[1] Here, then, we have a swarthy *jongleur*, or *joculator*, who was also a fortune-teller, in third-century England. And there is no reason to suppose that he was the only "Æthiop" among his brother minstrels. It is true that he appears as the follower of an invader, but that fact does not render it necessary to believe that there were no black-skinned jongleurs in England before the

[1] Ritson's *Annals of the Caledonians, etc.*, pp. 61, 62. Edinburgh, 1828.

third century. At any rate, he is a very interesting specimen of the early juggler; and one would like to know what was the language spoken by himself and his brother Ethiopians. The story retold by Ritson makes him speak Latin; but was that his mother tongue?

One might indulge still further in speculations regarding the antiquity of gypsy-minstrelsy in Europe. It has been pointed out to me that Liszt (*Des Bohémiens, et de leur Musique en Hongrie*) has styled certain of his compositions "Hungarian *Rhapsodies*," because they contain a certain element (giving a character to the whole) which strongly reminded him of the ancient Greek Rhapsody. And he acknowledges that these "Hungarian Rhapsodies" are largely the result of his intercourse with the *gypsies* of Hungary. Now, it has further been pointed out to me that the early rhapsodists of Greece were nomadic ballad-singers, like those people whom we call *gypsies* when they are spoken of in comparatively recent times, and *jugglers*, or *jongleurs*, at earlier dates. Further, those ancient rhapsodists, or ballad-singers, employed a certain recitative chant, as did also the later rhapsodists of Ireland; while one of the names lately given to gypsies was that of "the *canting* crew."[1] The *Sibyls* of antiquity, also, are

[1] See *Ancient and Modern Britons*, vol. ii. p. 290, *note*, and pp. 300, 301.

regarded by Mr. Paul Bataillard as, in all probability, of gypsy race.[1] These last, however, are here cited for the sake of indicating a caste of possible gypsies, at a remote date; and not as examples of wandering musicians.

In these statements and suggestions bearing upon "the gypsies as musicians," there is much that does not strictly belong to Professor De Goeje's theme; and perhaps there is also a good deal that would not commend itself to him. But, though somewhat speculative, the ideas thrown out in this note seem to me to be worth considering.

The following reference bears upon the remarks made regarding gypsies in their character of *jugglers*, not where that word signifies *musicians*, but where it denotes *mountebanks*. A writer of last century, in stating that it is a gypsy maxim to "beg when people's hearts are merry," adds that this is "also the practice of mountebanks, who are of the same origin with the gypsies," and whose custom it is to "put the people always in good humour by jokes, by tricks and tumblings, before they offer to vend their medicines." The people whom he calls "mountebanks" are thus made to combine in themselves the characteristics of *gypsies*, *joculatores*, *sleight-of-hand performers*, *acrobats*, and *quacks*, or *charlatans*. So that any collected proofs, or hints, of the connection between gypsies and

[1] See *Les Origines des Bohémiens*, pp. 19, 20.

those itinerant castes would have been quite superfluous to this author, to whom that connection was an accepted fact. [The passage quoted is from a curious work—*Mammuth; or Human Nature Displayed . . . in a Tour with the Tinkers:* London, 1789 (see pp. 97, 98, vol. i.). Its author, a Dr. Thomson, had plainly gone through experiences similar to those of Borrow and others, and although the book is largely Gulliverian and fanciful, many of the statements about *British* gypsies seem to be reliable.]

NOTE Q.—*Zigeuners, Zigani, etc.*

With so many hypotheses before one—each in its turn appearing to be the most plausible—it is difficult to know which one to favour. It may be further noted, that, in addition to the derivations suggested by Professor De Goeje, and many others, Mr. C. G. Leland has lately propounded another solution of "this philological *ignis fatuus*" (in *The Gypsies*, p. 339, *et seq.*).

PLAN OF BHURTPOOR.

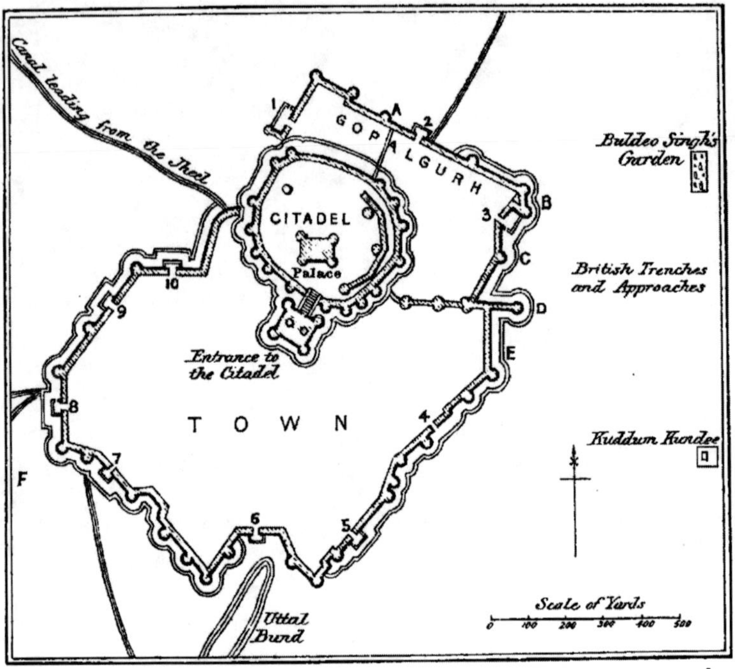

1 GOPALGURH GATE
2 JUNGEENAH GATE
3 SOORAJPORE GATE
4 MUTTRA GATE
5 BEERNARAIN GATE
6 UTTAL-BUND GATE
7 NEEMDAH GATE
8 ANAH GATE
9 KOMBHEER GATE
10 BANSOO GATE

A **Breach assaulted by Lt.-Col. Delamain.**
B **General Reynell's Main Attack.**
C **Colonel Wilson's Attack.**
D **General Nicholls' Main Attack.**
E **Extreme Left Breach.**
F **Site of Lord Lake's Batteries (1804-5).**

1 Assault on the "long-necked" bastion by General Nicholls' main column.

2 Colonel Wilson's escalade.

3 The Patha

THE STORMING

(SHOWING THE NORTH EASTERN PORTIONS O

J. Bartholomew, Edin.

...ion attacked by General Reynell's main column

4 Colonel Delamain's assault.

... BHURTPOOR.

... ENCEINTE, WHERE THE ATTACK WAS MADE.)

THE SIEGE OF BHURTPOOR.

"THE traditions of the Hindu Játs of Biána and Bharatpur point to Kandahar as their parent country," we are told by a well-known Indian archæologist—General Cunningham. Whether this town is the modern *Kandahar*, or whether it is that *Gandâra*, *Kandohâr*, or *Kondohâr*, to which Professor De Goeje refers, is a question requiring little more than a passing allusion here. But those Jauts of Bhurtpoor (otherwise *Bharatpur*, *Bhartpur*, and *Bhurtpore*) are undoubtedly an offshoot from the great Jaut or Zott stem, whose history has been so closely studied by the Dutch gypsiologist. And to British readers they have quite a peculiar interest. Because it was from the walls of their fortress that a British army was compelled, in the January of 1805, to retire, baffled and humbled, after vainly attempting on four different occasions to carry the place by storm; and although, twenty-one years later, this failure was balanced by the triumphant assault directed by Lord Combermere, the victory was not obtained until after a stubborn and masterly defence, by a most gallant foe.

That this particular Jaut family was seated in Afghanistan at an earlier date is not unlikely; and there are still many of their kindred in that country. "The Jats of Afghanistan," says one writer,[1] "doubtless belong to the same vast race as the Jats and Jâts who form so large a part of the population of the territories now governed from Lahore and Karachi." These Afghan Jauts are described as "a fine, athletic, dark, handsome race;" and, together with the *Hindkis*,

[1] In the *Encyclopædia Britannica* (9th edit.), vol. i. p. 235.

they constitute about one-eighth of the population of Afghanistan.

But, if the Jauts of Bhurtpoor have come from the Kandahar of Afghanistan, their exodus must be placed five hundred years back, at least. Because Reinaud, as quoted by De Goeje, informs us that this tribe was settled in the neighbourhood of Delhi at the time of Tamerlane's invasion of the north of India. It is less likely, however, that their "parent country" was Kandahar than that it was Sind; in which latter territory the coinage of another town, Kandohâr, was current. And Sind, together with the Punjaub, was peculiarly the home of the Jauts. It was in the Indus Valley that Tamerlane slew two thousand of the race before he came to Delhi; it was this district, inclusive of the Five Rivers, that an early writer says was "of old" inhabited solely by people of Jaut blood; and so much was the identity of *Jaut* and *Sindi* recognized that the two terms were interchangeable, and the speech of the

Jauts is, we are told, "now generally known as Sindhî."[1]

Whatever their earlier history may have been, the Jauts of Bhurtpoor are discernible in that neighbourhood in the fourteenth century, the era of Tamerlane. And they have held their ground there ever since. At the present day, the population of the territory of Bhurtpoor, estimated at about 750,000, consists mainly of Jauts; and its princes, for many generations, have been of this stock.

This state, we learn, rose into importance in the early part of last century, "under

[1] It may be inferred, from two statements in Professor De Goeje's treatise, that *Sind* at one time included a large part of Modern Beloochistan. Thus, *Kozdur* is stated (*ante*, p. 9, note 5) to be situated in Sind, although it is really a considerable distance within the eastern frontier of Beloochistan. A much more extreme instance than this is the reference to the town of Tîz, or Teez, which is described as "the capital of Mokrân *in Sind*" (*ante*, pp. 25, 26), whereas Mokran, or Mekran, is wholly in Beloochistan, Teez itself being about four hundred miles west of Sind.

Súraj Mall, who bore a conspicuous part in the destruction of the Delhi empire. Having built the forts of Díg and Kumbher in 1730, he received, in 1756, the title of Rájá, and subsequently joined the great Marhattá army with 30,000 troops. But the misconduct of the Marhattá leader induced him to abandon the confederacy, just in time to escape the murderous defeat at Pániput. Súraj Mall raised the Ját power to its highest point;[1] and Colonel Dow, in 1770, estimated the Rájá's revenue (perhaps extravagantly) at £2,000,000, and his military force at 60,000 or 70,000 men. In 1803, the East India Company concluded a treaty, offensive and defensive, with Bhartpur. In 1804, however, the Rájá assisted the Marhattás against the British."[2] Then followed Lord Lake's campaign, at the outset of which he captured the fortress of Díg; but was never able to penetrate the formidable ramparts that sur-

[1] That is to say, in this locality.

[2] *Encyc. Brit.*, 9th edit. vol. iii., *Bhartpur.*

rounded the city of Bhurtpoor, in spite of many efforts, which cost him several thousands of men.

From that date up to the year 1826, this fortress was regarded by the natives of India as impregnable; and, moreover, as being the very citadel of India, in which centred all their hopes of ultimate British overthrow. In its widest sense, "Bhurtpoor" signifies a district of about the same extent as Lincolnshire, in which, at that time, were situated not only the large fortified city of the same name, but also the strongholds of Deig, Biana, Weer, and Combheer. But these latter depended for their integrity upon the great central fortress; and when our troops entered them after that had fallen, they met with no resistance from the various garrisons. Thus, it was the great city itself that was actually "Bhurtpoor." And this place, although considerably strengthened after Lake's repulse, had been regarded as practically impregnable for a very long period;

not only so far back as the days of Súraj Mall, but long before that. "For centuries many other threatened states had, it was said, sent their stores to this stronghold of India for safety."[1] And this feeling of confidence was, naturally, not lessened after 1805. "Its imagined impregnability had been confirmed, in the opinion of the natives, by the repeated failures of the gallant army under Lord Lake. 'Oh, you may bully us; but go and take Bhurtpore,' was a common expression among the petty chiefs and refractory rajahs we had frequently to reduce."[2]

[1] Lord Combermere's *Memoirs*, vol. ii. p. 236. London, 1866.

[2] *Ibid.*, p. 237. Sir Thomas Seaton testifies to the same feeling among the peasantry. "As my regiment approached Agra," he says, in describing his march to Bhurtpoor, "escorting the guns from Meerut, we heard, as we passed through the various villages, the confident predictions muttered by the natives as to the fate that awaited us. 'Ah, go to Bhurtpoor; you won't come back!' said some, their wish, no doubt, father to the thought; and one old wrinkled hag, rushing out of her house and raising her skinny arms in the air, exclaimed, 'Go to Bhurtpoor; they'll split you up. Go and be

By 1825, the capture of this place had become necessary to British supremacy.

At this period an opportunity had presented itself for our interference. Two years previously, the old Rajah of Bhurtpoor had died childless, and the throne had been claimed by his brother and by the son of another brother. At first, the latter had to yield to his uncle, who, however, died within two years; poisoned, it is supposed, by his nephew, who then placed himself upon the throne. One account states that he had entered Bhurtpoor at the head of a body of troops, and killed the rajah; another version is that he, at that time, slew the then *regent*, the rajah having previously been poisoned. At any rate, he made himself Rajah of Bhurtpoor, and seized the person of the acknowledged sovereign, a boy of five years old—son of the murdered rajah. The name of this usurper was Doorjun Saul, and he,

killed, all of you'" (*From Cadet to Colonel*, vol. i. chap. iii. London, 1866).

and all that dynasty, belonged to the race of the Jauts.[1]

[1] The version of the story given by Sir Thomas Seaton (*From Cadet to Colonel*, vol. i. chap. iii.) is to this effect. Sir David Ochterlony, acting for the Governor-General, had resolved to oust Doorjun Saul from the position he had gained, and, with this view, he assembled as large a force as he could, including a powerful train of artillery, and advanced towards Bhurtpoor. But the Governor-General, fearing "another war at a time when the resources of the empire were strained to the uttermost to maintain the contest with the Court of Ava," "gave orders for suspending the march of the troops, and as Doorjun Saul cunningly renounced his intention of usurping the throne, the soldiers were ordered to return to their cantonments." "No sooner were the troops dispersed, than Doorjun Saul, having succeeded in blinding the Governor-General's eyes, improved the opportunity of which, by the incapacity and want of judgment of his opponents, he was enabled to avail himself. He levied troops, laid in provisions, manufactured tons of powder and thousands of shot, repaired the ruinous walls of Bhurtpoor, cleared out the ditches, and strengthened all the works of that grand fortress; then he entered into negotiations with all the independent princes; and, entertaining and enrolling all the malcontents and turbulent spirits in the surrounding districts who flocked to his standard, he raised the military ardour of the Jats [described by Seaton as "a peculiar caste of people who inhabit that country"] by tales of former conquest and

It does not appear that the British authorities were actuated by any high moral motives in interfering at this point. It is true that the boy-rajah and his father before him had been formally recognized by us as the rightful rulers of Bhurtpoor. But then, Bhurtpoor had never acknowledged our right to settle its affairs; and, indeed, had dismissed us very summarily from its presence. However, it was convenient for us to regard this Doorjun Saul as a "usurper," and to despatch an army against him, with the ostensible object of displacing him and re-establishing the authority of his youthful cousin. This, indeed, was actually done—to outward appearance. But there was a vital difference between the position of the new rajah and that of his predecessors. These had been independent princes, and their principality was the heart of India. But the

hopes of future victory, and prepared to defend desperately the fortress that was considered by the whole of Hindostan as the impregnable bulwark against which the British power was destined to be broken."

reduction of Bhurtpoor made that province a dependency of the British Empire, and thenceforward its rajahs owned an allegiance that their predecessors would have scorned. There was a strong element of mockery in the "re-instatement" of this boy-rajah. His city was in the hands of the British, his territory was overrun by their troops, his own treasury was despoiled to the extent of £480,000 (not to speak of other forms of "loot"). And the British commander was enriched by £60,000; his officers and men receiving proportionate shares of the plunder. The way in which this was explained to be righteous cannot bear criticism.[1] But any

[1] On one page (p. 42) of the book from which I learn these facts (Lord Combermere's *Memoirs*, vol. ii.), this Doorjun Saul is spoken of as a "usurper," and it was because he was such that we dethroned him—or, rather, that is the reason we gave for our attack upon Bhurtpoor. But when all the wealth of Bhurtpoor fell to our disposal, it was not assigned to the young heir and his people. It all (or, at least, something like half a million in money and spoil) went into *our own* pockets. And this is the kind of defence we made: "*The fact of Doorjun Sal*

such virtuous explanation of our attitude is both hypocritical and unnecessary. The capture of Bhurtpoor was only a repetition of the old story of conquest and spoliation. Possibly the people of the Bhurtpoor territory *having been in quiet possession of the throne, and acknowledged by all parties in the state as the maharajah, no individual either openly or secretly supporting the claims of Bulwunt Singh* (the boy-rajah), *naturally gave the former the full right to all the property in the fort, and deprived the latter of any claim which he might be supposed to have to it*" (p. 130). This sentence is one continuous contradiction of our alleged motives throughout the affair. Our *real* motive can be seen from these words (p. 62): "The capture of Bhurtpore was regarded by the princes of India as the test of our power, and a failure would have been the signal for a general outbreak and the formation of a powerful confederacy against us." And when one reads that "on the 24th [January, 1826], Lord Combermere was able to report the complete subjugation of the whole of the Bhurtpore territory," one must understand that it was subdued, not in the interests of the young rajah, but of the British Empire. The succeeding sentence, which states that "the young rajah . . . was formally reinstated . . . on the musnud, from which he had been temporarily driven," is not only a flat contradiction of the argument advanced in the sentence given in italics above, but it is only half true. He was not *reinstated*.

held different opinions as to who was their rightful rajah; but that was a private affair. They were quite unanimous in resisting to the uttermost all attempts at British invasion. Bhurtpoor was not besieged in order to settle a question of succession: the struggle was a contest between its people and the successful invaders—with India and Britain looking on.

It was on this important point, then, that the British forces converged, in the second week of the December of 1825; the right wing, with the commander-in-chief, advancing from Muttra, and the left wing marching from Agra. The composition of this army was partly British, partly Native, and the total number of men was over 27,000, afterwards increased by reinforcements to about 29,000. On the 11th of December, the investment of the city was completed; the cordon of the besiegers being fourteen and a half miles in length, though on the western side this was little more than a chain of cavalry posts.

The position and appearance of the beleaguered city is thus described: "Bhurtpore, situated about thirty miles to the west of Agra, stands in the midst of an almost level plain. The town, eight miles in circumference, is bounded on the western side by a ridge of low, bare, flat rocks, while everywhere else its limits are dotted by a few isolated eminences of little height or size." That the surrounding country was not wholly characterized by the arid appearance suggested in Captain Field's sketch,[1] as well as by the above sentence, may be seen from this description given by a young officer, who was at the time one of a reconnoitring party, then advancing through "the forest that lay between our camp and the town." "We entered a beautiful glade, fine soft grass under our feet, noble trees of all kinds on each side, and in such varieties and luxuriance as only a tropical country can show. In the distance, and at the end of the glade, rose

[1] Introduced between pp. 180 and 181.

a round tower, with some other loopholed building,"—a corner of the fortifications of Bhurtpoor. "A part of the country surrounding the town," says another writer, "was covered by thick wood and jungle, the remainder by ruined villages, small gardens, and enclosures."

Of the citadel and fortifications, some idea is gained from the plan attached to Lord Combermere's *Memoirs*;[1] as well as from Captain Field's sketch of the north-eastern corner of the ramparts. The account given in the *Memoirs* is as follows:—

"The fortifications consist of a citadel and a continuous enceinte of thirty-five lofty mud bastions, connected by curtains, and in shape generally either semicircular or like the frustra of cones. On some of these bastions there are cavaliers, and most of them are joined to the curtains by long narrow necks. Additions have been made to the enceinte

[1] A representation of which is given between pp. 180 and 181.

since Lord Lake's time, and one bastion, called the Futteh Boorj, or Bastion of Victory, was vauntingly declared to have been built with the blood and bones of those who fell in the last siege.[1] In many cases the ramparts were strengthened by several rows of trunks of trees, which were buried upright in the mass of earth, and all of them were constructed of clay mixed with straw and cow-dung. This composition had been put on in layers, each of which was allowed to harden under the fierce sun before another layer was added. Such a mode of

[1] "Had not the Jats at Bhurtpoor erected the Futteh Boorg, or Bastion of Victory, in which were built up the skulls and bones of the thousands of the dreaded gora log (white men) who had fallen in Lord Lake's vain attempt to storm the bulwark of Hindostan? Was not the great and terrible Lony Ochter (Ochterlony), in whom they had the discernment to see their most formidable enemy, dead? Were not their works higher and stronger than they had ever been before, and was not the Motee Jheel (lake), from the abundant rains sent by the Gods, full of water, which, when they had let it into the ditch, who would dare to attack them with any hope of success?" (Seaton's *From Cadet to Colonel*).

construction rendered any attempt to establish a practicable breach almost impossible; and we have seen that, from the shape of the bastions, enfilade was in many cases very difficult. The enceinte was surrounded by a broad and deep ditch, from twenty to thirty feet long [? broad]. This was, in fact, a nullah, or dry watercourse, which, running through stiff clay, had steep, almost perpendicular, banks. One source of weakness, however, attached to this ravine, which arose from the numerous small watercourses leading into it, affording in many places an easy descent. Outside the nine gates were an equal number of semicircular earthworks." So much for the outer ramparts: there yet remained the interior stronghold, situated in the northern part of the town. "The citadel, completely commanding the body of the place, was of very great strength, rising to a height above the level of the ground of one hundred and fourteen feet. The ditch, a hundred and fifty feet broad, and fifty-nine deep, had its counterscarp faced by a perpendicular revetment of stone. From the bottom of the escarp rose a perpendicular stone wall of eighty feet, forming a fausse-braye, well flanked by forty semicircular towers. Above this arose another stone wall, seventy-four feet in height, and flanked by eleven conical bastions,[1] whose total relief reached one hundred and seventy-three feet." In the centre of this citadel stood the rajah's palace and harem. "The strength of Bhurtpore was further increased by the Moti Jheel, a lake situated at a short distance from the place. This lake was bounded on the side of the town by a bund or embankment, by cutting which, as was actually done during the former siege, not only, as we have said

[1] Although the citadel was largely built of stone, it would seem that its towers and bastions were constructed much after the fashion of the ramparts that girdled the town, viz. of bricks, overlain with a thick casing of concrete. This is to be assumed from a reference made to "those huge mud mounds of the citadel," in Lord Combermere's *Memoirs* (vol. ii. p. 292).

before, could the ditch [the dry moat surrounding the enceinte] be filled, but also a great portion of the surrounding country placed under water." Finally, the fortifications all round bristled with artillery, to furnish which "tons of powder and thousands of shot" had been duly provided; and the heavier fire of the cannons and "jinjalls" could be supplemented by the rattle of countless matchlocks; while, in case of a night attack, the whole line of the ramparts could be brilliantly and instantaneously lighted up with Bengal lights. And the men who defended these massive walls were twenty-five thousand strong, of warlike Jaut and Pathan strain, brave and resolute as their assailants, and confident in the memory of their past victories. That Combermere would conquer where Lake had failed, was by no means a foregone conclusion; and the task before him was great indeed.

These, briefly enough described, were the defences of Bhurtpoor. But, besides the armed inhabitants, who constituted the garrison, the town which these wide walls enclosed contained a population of a hundred thousand people. Its appearance was presumably that of any other great Indian city at that date. One reads of verandahed houses, and gardens, and of the maharajah's palace, with its marble roof. One reads, above all, of its wealth: "As we before stated, a belief that incalculable treasure was concealed beneath the fortress of Bhurtpore generally prevailed in the East. For centuries many other threatened states had, it was said, sent their stores to this stronghold of India for safety. Its sovereigns, belonging to a predatory tribe [the Jauts], were also supposed themselves to have amassed plunder which they dared not acknowledge, and knew not how to expend."[1] It was even stated that the amount of treasure there amassed, "in specie and jewels," was "said to exceed £30,000,000 sterling."[2] It is at least certain that £480,000

[1] Combermere's *Memoirs*, vol. ii. p. 236. [2] *Ibid.*, p. 239.

(in money and valuables) fell into British hands, while we are told that "immense treasures" were secretly carried off by the female inhabitants, who were allowed to pass out through the British lines as the investment became closer. On another occasion, also, "a large body of the enemy's cavalry, laden, as is supposed, with treasure," sallied out of the fortress, and succeeded in forcing their way through the lines of the besiegers. Moreover, it was alleged that the men of one of our regiments had their musket-barrels filled with coins when they left the conquered city; and there is every hint that "looting" went on on all sides, over and above what was formally acknowledged. "Amongst other plunder at Bhurtpore," writes Lord Combermere to his sister, "I have got some beautiful old armour, which was taken one hundred years ago by a Bhurtpore rajah from Agra, and belonged to the famous Ackbar." Still more interesting and suggestive is his mention of "a very curious and handsome Bhurtpore book . . . much prized by all oriental scholars in Calcutta," which also formed a portion of the general's spoil. And none of this was included in the portion of £60,000 allotted to him. With a general so free from scruple in his mode of "reinstating" the displaced Rajah of Bhurtpoor, it is likely that a very large amount of unacknowledged treasure was distributed throughout the besieging army.

Of the appearance of the garrison, we get an interesting and picturesque account from Sir Thomas Seaton, then a young cadet—receiving his "baptism of fire." In the following sentences, he is describing a reconnaisance made, in the earlier stage of the siege, by a "feeling party," under the direction of General Nicholls, young Seaton being, of course, one of their number :—

. . . "We now formed into line, and, advancing through the forest, came all at once into the open, and Bhurtpoor burst on our view not three hundred yards off. The scene was beautiful in the extreme. Two lofty massive towers on the left—one that of the celebrated Futteh Boorj (Bastion of Victory), built by the Jats to commemorate Lord Lake's repulse—seemed to form an angle of the fort, at a point from which a succession of equally massive bastions and curtains crossed our front, and continued off to the right, until a projecting bastion, meeting a part of the forest, cut all further view.

"The embrasures were armed with guns, and on the walls were assembled a great number of the garrison, standing or reclining in every sort of careless attitude. Some were sitting cross-legged, with their matchlocks over their knees; others with their legs dangling over the walls; while many, with their sword and shield in hand, or their matchlock over their shoulders, were standing upon the parapets, apparently talking and chatting at ease, little suspecting that an enemy was so near.

"The walls were sharply and clearly defined against the blue and cloudless sky, and the sun at our backs threw into high relief the wild-looking soldiery on the parapets, in their quaint and picturesque costumes, lighting up the varied colours of their Eastern garb with a flood of glorious sunshine, which made their brightly polished arms glitter like diamonds.

"Several groups of men, whom we observed sitting together, were singing in chorus, beating time with their hands, and here and there along the walls a tall spear, stuck upright, bore a little pennon, the mark, probably, of some petty chief.

"The overhanging boughs of the thick forest trees formed a shade which partially screened our dark uniforms, and for a minute or two we were unobserved. The reconnaissance was nearly completed, when the beauty and interest of the scene were greatly enhanced by the appearance, from between the two bastions on our left, of a clump of horsemen, prancing and caracolling, each with a bright matchlock over his shoulder, or a long spear in his hand.

"On they came bounding towards us, till their progress was arrested by our horse artillery, who, quick as thought, unlimbered, and in a few seconds sent a couple of shots right through the capering steeds and horsemen, scattering them right and left, and unhorsing many of the best riders among them.

"When the men on the walls saw the flash and heard the sound of our guns, there was, in the first moment of surprise, a tremendous hubbub; then down came a perfect shower of shot and grape and matchlock-balls. The enemy had evidently laid their guns for the edge of the forest and been practising at it, for almost as quickly as I can write the word, eleven of our men were knocked over, and the whole force was exposed to so sharp a fire that General Nicholls ordered us to disperse and shelter ourselves wherever we could."[1]

The "quaint and picturesque costumes" of the garrison, and "the varied colours of their Eastern garb," are casually referred to in an account of the grand assault: "Alarmed at the event [the firing of the mines], the garrison crowded the angle of the north-east bastion, and could be seen, dressed either in white or brightly coloured garments, some waving their swords in defiance, others beckoning eagerly for support."[2] In Captain Field's picture, however, the very same people are represented as wearing blue uniforms, which is not consistent with the expression "white or brightly coloured garments." But the defenders of the north-east bastion, eight hundred in number, were Pathans,[3] and, whatever their attire, it cannot be regarded as exemplifying the fashions of

[1] *From Cadet to Colonel*, vol. i. chap. iii. London, 1866.

[2] Combermere's *Memoirs*, vol. ii. p. 113.

[3] *Ibid.*, p. 125.

the *Jauts*. Thus, the picturesque soldiers of whom Seaton speaks may have differed very considerably from those Pathans, as regards their costume. And the former were presumably Jauts; those of them, at any rate, that manned the battlements of the Futteh Boorj, since that was the *Jauts*' "Bastion of Victory." So also must have been the cavalry spoken of by Seaton in the above passage; who, it may be supposed, resembled —or were identical with—the Jaut horsemen described by him on a previous occasion, in these words: "Amongst the enemy's horsemen were numbers who were clad in suits of chain-mail, through which our lancers could not drive their lances, but which the bayonets of the 14th went through as if it had been paper, the fine point of the bayonet and the heavy weight of the musket overcoming all the resistance of the finely tempered armour." Not at all a bad picture of Saracenic knighthood must those Eastern horsemen have presented, with their chain-armour, pennoned lances, swords, and shields; nor was the long matchlock on their shoulders the least out of keeping with the term "Saracen."[1] For the use of firearms is quite a modern affair in Europe, when compared with Asia; and the "Saracens" (a somewhat vague expression) are understood to have taught the manufacture of gunpowder, and of artillery of all kinds, to the ruder races of the West.

These descriptions are here quoted because they relate to the people with whom we are most concerned in these pages—the Jauts of Bhurtpoor. To what extent the people of that city were of other lineage is not known to the writer. But the ruling race had for

[1] Two years later, Lord Combermere received from the Rajah of Pattialah "a complete suit of chain-armour, with casque and gauntlets of steel, inlaid with gold, a sword and shield, a bow and arrows, and a dagger." It is likely that the "beautiful old armour" which he carried off from Bhurtpoor "amongst other plunder," was of this description; and that many such were then in daily use in that stronghold of the East.

a long time been that of the Jauts, and as they figure particularly in the initial act of the defence of Bhurtpoor, so also are they visible to the very last scene of the struggle.

Mention has been made of a lake situated near the town on its western side, which communicated, by means of a canal, with the moat which surrounded Bhurtpoor. Both moat and canal were kept dry, except when a siege was threatened; and then, by cutting the embankment of the lake, these were filled, and even much of the surrounding land placed under water. The Jaut cavalry were just in the act of cutting this embankment, prior to the investment, when a detachment of horse belonging to Lord Combermere's left wing came upon the scene, and the enemy, taken by surprise, had to give way, after an imperfect resistance. Had the advance of the British forces been delayed by a few hours, the task before Lord Combermere would have been ten times as difficult. Because the walls of the fortress would only yield to mining;[1] and, moreover, a wide stretch of water and swamp would have prevented the besieging forces from making any near approach to the fortress, had the waters of the lake been let loose a few hours sooner.

The details of the siege are so well described elsewhere, that there seems little excuse for repeating them here. On both sides there were brave men and skilful warriors; but even Bhurtpoor had to yield at last to the persistent and masterly efforts of Combermere.[2] The struggle began on

[1] "They present a strange and gigantic concrete of earth even to-day," says Sir William Gomm, writing from Bhurtpoor in 1851, "manifesting how proof it was against battery to any extent, and only to be disturbed by the mine."

[2] A story is told in the *Memoirs* which is characteristic both of the great duke and the leader whom he chose. When an expedition against Bhurtpoor had been decided upon in the year 1825, the Directors of the East India Company sent a deputation to the Duke of Wellington, "in order that he might indicate to them a commander likely to accomplish what even the victorious Lake had been unable to effect. In answer to their inquiries as to

the morning of the 10th of December, 1825, when the Jauts were foiled in their attempt to let loose the waters of the lake. On the following day the investment of the fortress was completed; the left wing, under General Nicholls, having then joined with the other division, which, with the Commander-in-Chief, had come up on the 10th. During the next nine days, the time of the British commander was taken up in examining the ground and maturing his plan of attack; the troops being employed in reconnoitring, in throwing up defensive works, and in making the necessary gabions and fascines (some of which

whom his Grace considered the most fitting person, he replied—

"'You can't do better than have Lord Combermere. He's the man to take Bhurtpore;' or words of a similar purport.

"'But,' urged the deputation, 'we don't think very highly of Lord Combermere. In fact, we do not consider him a man of any great genius.'

"'I don't care a d—n about his genius, I tell you he's the man to take Bhurtpore!' exclaimed the duke to his astonished auditors." And the sequel showed him to be right.

figure conspicuously in the foreground of Captain Field's sketch). A system of signalling was also established between the various posts forming the investment, and a line was formed to enable due notice to be given of the departure of the frequent bodies of cavalry which the garrison of the neighbouring fortified town of Kombheer sent out to the assistance of their beleaguered friends. These mounted parties, we are told, "interrupted our communications, carried off our horses, cut off our camp followers, and generally did much damage."[1] Skirmishes with these outsiders were thus of frequent occurrence, and the garrison of Bhurtpoor were ever on the watch to harass their foe, not only by the fire of their heavy guns

[1] They are spoken of (*Memoirs*, vol. ii. p. 55) as "flying parties of Ja*l* horsemen;" but, although this word *Jal* is frequently used by the same writers, it seems that *Jat* is intended, but is misspelt by a clerical or printer's error. It is obvious that this is the case when Khoosial Singh, brother-in-law of the usurping rajah, is styled (p. 118) "the gallant *Jal*."

and lighter firearms from the walls of their fortress, but also by means of flying parties of horsemen and sharpshooters.

In order to deceive the enemy, the British general continued, as long as possible, to feign that the assault was to be made from the south-west, where Lake had vainly made the attempt. And, with this expectation, that portion of the fortifications had been greatly strengthened. But when, on the 23rd of December, the cordon of investment was drawn tighter, and our troops seized and occupied two positions on the *eastern* side of the city, not eight hundred yards from its ramparts, then the real design of the besiegers was suspected. The two captured positions were, a small village and —about eight hundred yards further north— the garden of the ex-rajah, beside which were a ruined temple and a flat-roofed house, thenceforth the point of observation of the British general. On these two positions, then, a heavy fire was directed from the walls, during the whole of this 23rd of December. This, however, did little harm, as the guns on the walls could not be sufficiently depressed. Of much more importance were the bodies of cavalry and sharpshooters which were sent out to harass the defenders of this newly acquired position. "To check these incursions, a rough breast-work of cotton bales was hastily set up, under shelter of which two six-pounder guns and a twelve-pounder howitzer opened on the enemy, and, aided by the fire of some Goorkha skirmishers, soon cleared the esplanade." In the evening, the first parallel was traced, at a distance of six hundred yards from the walls, and stretching from the front of the captured village to the ruined temple beside the garden of the former rajah.

But the defenders of Bhurtpoor never lost an opportunity of harassing their assailants. The "great bundles of brushwood and bottomless baskets" (as the Bhurtpooreans styled the "fascines and gabions" of military phraseology), which formed the rudiments of the besiegers' batteries, offered continual "practice" to the artillery of the defenders. Seaton tells of his first experience of this on a certain moonlight night, when he and his company were employed in the construction of the left battery. A heavy fire had just been opened on them from the walls. "I was wondering," says the young cadet, "what mischief made the gabions dance about as they did; and, seeing some of the men sheltering themselves in the trench after laying down their loads, I was walking up to see if any one was amongst the gabions, when the motive-power was suddenly revealed to my weak mind by a large jinjall-ball (jinjall is a wall piece), which, as it went on its errand of destruction, caught the nearest gabion and knocked it over. As two or three more balls came whistling past my ears, I thought it prudent to walk over to the trench, and get sharply under cover. . . ."

Nor was the night which followed the forward movement of 23rd December allowed to pass without another attempt to oust us from our new position. For a sortie from the fortress was planned and partly carried out; but no actual engagement took place, the enemy retiring on discovering that we were in force.

On the morning of the 24th, the bombardment began in earnest; the initiative being taken by the besiegers, who, from two batteries completed during the night, opened fire with cannon and howitzer upon the ramparts, the citadel, and the town. And the defenders could do little in the way of retaliation, as, owing to the nearness of our batteries, the guns upon the walls of Bhurtpoor could not be depressed sufficiently to cause us any great injury. The havoc wrought by our shells among the defenceless townspeople was great. The compilers of Lord Combermere's *Memoirs* think it necessary to offer some apology for his action in this detail; but it is hardly necessary to repeat these apologies to a generation which has tolerated the bombardments of Paris and of Alexandria. Moreover, the effects of these casual bombshells in Bhurtpoor cannot have equalled in condensed butchery the results of the mines which were sprung on the day of the final assault, to be shortly noticed. But, so long as war is war, it is absurd to distinguish between one kind of slaughter and another. With regard to the bombs thrown in among the streets of Bhurtpoor, however, it is only right to notice that Lord Combermere gave the Jaut rajah every opportunity to save the women and children; and on the 24th "all the women not belonging to the royal family" (a reservation made, apparently, by the rajah himself) passed out from the city and through our lines, without molestation. On which occasion, it is said, they took with them a great quantity of the treasures of Bhurtpoor. An additional instalment of treasure was also, it is supposed, borne off on the following day; when a large body of cavalry broke out from the fortress, forced their way through our lines, and escaped out into the open country.[1]

Christmas Day was celebrated by "a heavy fire of shot, shrapnel, and shell," by which "much damage" was done to the fortifications of Bhurtpoor; and on the following day our fire was so heavy as to silence completely the opposing guns. On the 27th, the second parallel was begun, at a distance of two hundred and fifty yards

[1] On the night of the 27th, also, an attempt of the same kind was made, but without success. On that evening, between eight and nine o'clock, two hundred horsemen emerged from the Uttal-Bund gate, at the southern point of Bhurtpoor, "and after feeling the picquet on the Anah road, fell back under the walls of the fort until eleven o'clock, when they endeavoured to force their way by the Kombeer road, and between the villages of Murwarra and Bussie. They were obliged to retire in the direction of the fort, with the loss of thirty or forty men killed, fifteen wounded, and one hundred and seven prisoners; ten or twelve succeeded in forcing their way through a part of the camp."

from the moat. And on the 28th, the British coil was drawn still closer, our "approaches" being on that day within forty yards of the moat. So near were our batteries at this point, and so galling was our fire, that, on the next day, an envoy came out on behalf of six hundred of the garrison, who alleged that they had been recruited in our provinces, and now desired to be allowed to pass out through our lines. This offer, however, came to nothing, as they would not accept the conditions proposed to them—that they should lay down their arms, and become prisoners of war.

But, in spite of these waverers, and of the horsemen who had escaped a few days previously, the bulk of the twenty-five thousand that constituted the garrison of Bhurtpoor, fought on bravely to the end.[1] And, at this

[1] We read in Lord Combermere's *Memoirs* (vol. ii. p. 85) that, on the 10th of January, "a flag of protection was hoisted for the guidance of such of the inhabitants as might choose to leave the town. About seventy-two of the garrison had, during the preceding twenty-four

time, the end was still three weeks off. Indeed, this siege would have ended as Lake's did, had our troops depended only on the work wrought by our breaching batteries. These alone would never have made a way for the British troops. "Proof against battery to any extent, and only to be disturbed by the mine," was the verdict afterwards pronounced upon the "strange and gigantic concrete of earth" that encircled the city of Bhurtpoor. And this is the evidence given by one of those who fought in the left wing, under Nicholls: "The left breaching battery, which was armed with fourteen guns, opened fire, I think, on the 28th December; but after battering the curtain for a week, it was found impracticable to make a breach. The walls being of tough tenacious clay, which a shot would enter, pounding that particular spot to dust, but

hours, either surrendered or endeavoured to escape." Defections such as these, however, must have been comparatively few.

leaving the whole surrounding part uninjured as before, a lot of the upper part of the rampart came down, forming a fine slope of dust and clods, ready to deaden the force of any shots fired into it. After the place was taken, I lived for a week in a garden just behind the curtain that had been battered, and saw with my own eyes that there then was no practicable breach. I also remarked that the men who were digging out the shot could with difficulty ascend the battered place, even after much had been dug down. Our tactics, therefore, were changed."[1]

"On the 6th [January, 1826], it was decided that the results of the breaching batteries were not such that reliance could be placed on them alone. Lord Combermere, therefore, resolved to give time for the action of the mines."[2] The making of these mines had been commenced on the last

[1] Seaton's *From Cadet to Colonel*, vol. i. chap. iii.

[2] Lord Combermere's *Memoirs*, vol. ii. p. 79.

day of 1825, and the work had gone on continuously since then. Nor were the enemy idle, in this respect, either. And the two hostile forces were busy as moles, mining and countermining, during the rest of the siege. But the defenders were outmanœuvred by their foes.

Although Combermere was now relying wholly on this arm of his service for the final victory, yet the artillery duel continued throughout the remainder of the struggle. A passage of Seaton's, relating to this time, deserves quotation here:—

"On the night of the 7th of January, just after dusk, a shot from the fort blew up one of our tumbrils proceeding to the trenches with powder. The fire was communicated to one of our magazines, containing 20,000 lbs. of powder, which instantly exploded, and set fire to a quantity of engineers' stores. The awful crash turned us all out, and we went to the front to see what was going on. As our camp was on a rather rising ground, we could just see the line of the walls of Bhurtpoor over the tops of the forest-trees, and when we came to the front we at once perceived a tremendous blaze from the burning stores; and the smoke being blown aside by a gentle breeze, the whole line of fortifications was seen brilliantly lighted up with large Bengal lights, evidently prepared against a night attack. At the same time, every gun that would bear on our trenches opened fire, and many that could not joined the cannonade, just for the sake of the row they made. Every jinjall and matchlock was pointed at us, and a heavy fire was maintained all along the walls. It was a magnificent scene, the red flames of the burning stores lighting up the forest, and the Bengal lights burnt by the enemy making the long line of fortification shine like silver. The broad blaze of the guns, and the rapid sparkling of musketry, formed a display of fireworks such as I have seldom seen equalled.

"Our astonishment was great at the silence of our batteries, which, as we afterwards learned, was purposely maintained, with the view of saving our men. When the enemy got tired with their exertions, our mortar batteries began to speak out, first one shell being seen in the air, then two, and then whole flights, bursting in the town with terrible precision. All night this deadly rain of shells continued, with a result which might be conjectured from the numerous conflagrations we witnessed. The fire had burst out in two or three places at once, and in the confusion which this must have occasioned within the walls, two brass 13-inch mortars arrived from Delhi, and opened upon the town. The first shell was aimed at the Rajah's Palace, and fell right into the marble enclosure on the top, where the Rajah was at the time in company with his wives. It went crashing through four thick stone floors, and burst in a room on the ground, to the terrible alarm, as we heard afterwards, of the ladies who witnessed it."[1]

This kind of warfare, then, was continued to the end, although the mining operations proceeded without intermission. Whenever it was thought that they might prove efficient, either in silencing the enemy's fire at those points where it was peculiarly harassing, or by effecting breaches in those obstinate concrete walls, additional batteries were from time to time erected by the British. And the heavy fire thus kept up must have wrought great damage. We learn from the *Memoirs* that "one thousand eight hundred and eight shot and shell were fired" from our lines on the 13th of January; that "on the 15th the batteries continued firing as

[1] *From Cadet to Colonel*, vol. i. chap. iii.

usual, and expended 1466 rounds of ammunition in the course of the twenty-four hours;" and that "on the 16th the batteries fired somewhat more heavily, discharging 1894 shot and shells." However, this could not have gone on much longer, because the final instalment of ammunition from the arsenal at Agra arrived in our camp on the 16th; and after that "there was not a single eighteen-pounder gun to be obtained higher up than Allahabad."

Sorties were, of course, made by the besieged at every available opportunity. On the 12th of January, a force of about fifteen hundred came out to attack our trenches, but these soon retired, seeing that our position was too strong. Two days later, a less vigorous attempt was easily foiled by a portion of General Nicholls's force. Other outbreaks had already taken place in December,[1] one on Christmas Day, when a body of cavalry succeeded in cutting its way through

[1] Referred to at p. 163, *ante*.

our lines; and another on the night of 27th December, though in this instance the Bhurtpooreans were nearly all captured or slain. In some cases, these sorties appear to have been made in the hope of inserting a wedge in our cordon, which, if pushed home by reinforcements from the garrison, would have divided our forces and opened up communication with the still-unconquered provincials of Bhurtpoor, who from their fortresses of Deeg, Biana, Weer, and Kombheer, continued to despatch flying parties to harass our rear and the weaker parts of our lines. And even if some of the Bhurtpoor garrison were actuated by the most selfish motives in thus trying to escape, their efforts, if successful, would promote the same end. But all attempts of this sort, whether from within Bhurtpoor, or from the open country, were unavailing.

Although the continuous cannonade from the fortifications, as well as that from the British batteries, formed a very important feature of the siege, the mines, as already stated, constituted the key of the situation. This fact had now been fully grasped by the British commander; and no time was lost in pushing on the works.

While working in their galleries beneath the counterscarp of the moat, on one occasion, the British miners and their opponents met face to face; and there being at that time only two of the enemy's miners in their gallery, they were easily secured, and the gallery itself (eighty feet in length) appropriated. This was on the 5th of January. On the 8th, three of these mines were exploded, "and an excellent descent into the ditch was thus formed." Another mine had been sprung on the previous day beneath the north-east bastion, but with little effect. Probably the captured gallery was not one of those blown up on the 8th, for we read that on the following night "it was determined to dislodge the enemy from a scarp gallery which our sappers had previously seized, but from which they had been compelled to retire." This was done by a volunteer party of eleven, who, entering the moat by the breach made on the preceding day, "cautiously approached the mouth of the gallery, carrying with them 350 lbs. of powder. On coming near to the spot, they heard the enemy's miners conversing merrily together inside, happily unconscious of the fate which awaited them. Forbearance, however, can find no place in that most ruthless of all modes of warfare—mining. The powder was laid, the fuse fired, and in an instant the gallery, with all its occupants, ceased to be."

Two days later, the British general sent a small party of Goorkhas to dislodge the enemy's miners, whom he perceived (no doubt, from his point of observation on the flat-roofed house) at work in the moat. The Goorkhas got into the moat, unseen by the enemy, but as they neared the gallery where the miners were at work, their presence was discovered. Although the Goorkhas only numbered seventeen, and the Bhurtpooreans were estimated at sixty, the latter fled hastily along the ditch, and through the gate (? the Soorajpore Gate) into the city; three of their number having fallen before the fusils of the Goorkhas.

These little Goorkhas (then, as now, among the very bravest men in our Indian army) distinguished themselves greatly on another occasion. It was rumoured that the breach made by General Nicholls's guns had subsequently been so trenched and defended, that, when the day of the assault should come, the onset of his troops would thus be altogether checked. Accordingly, a forlorn hope of about a dozen men, of whom four or five were Goorkhas (the rest being British, and including two officers), volunteered to ascertain the truth. In broad daylight, and with no scrap of shelter, this gallant little band advanced towards the rampart, and struggled up the almost perpendicular ascent, over mud, dust, and stone. And, although the walls above them were bristling with the spears and bayonets of the garrison, they were actually successful in gaining the summit unperceived and unmolested. Their sudden and unlooked-for appearance here amazed and confounded the Bhurtpooreans, who at once took them for the leaders of an attacking column. Before they could get over their surprise, this handful of heroes, with the most charming audacity, had given them a volley, delivered at the distance of only a few yards. And this they followed up with a shower of stones and dirt. But they did not remain long in this perilous position. A brief but comprehensive survey enabled them to take in the state of matters at this point of the fortification ; and then they turned, and fled rapidly down the steep banks of the breach. Had their retreat not been covered by a well-directed and constant fire of musketry from the trenches, which met the Bhurtpooreans the instant they showed themselves above the ramparts, the little band would have been at once annihilated. All but one, however, succeeded in gaining the British lines in safety; and not a moment too soon. For the garrison, "exasperated at their own loss, the escape of the party, and the impudence of the attempt, kept up such a tremendous discharge of all arms, matchlock, ginjal, cannon, etc., that for two hours not a man's head dare appear above the trench, unless he designed to be drilled like a colander." In this dashing affair, the chief actors were our own countrymen, but the historian is particular to note, here and elsewhere, the coolness and bravery of the Goorkhas.[1]

There is no room to refer at length to the other incidents of the siege: how one of our artillerymen deserted to the enemy, and, knowing Lord Combermere's daily movements, succeeded in sending a cannon-ball into the room he occupied in the house beside the rajah's garden; or how hopefulness and even merriment reigned in the British camp,

[1] These extracts are from Lord Combermere's *Memoirs*.

while from day to day despondency began to settle down upon the city of the Jauts. Nor can one speak particularly of the correspondence between Lord Combermere and the Rajah and Ranee, with reference to the safety of the women and children; although it may be noted that apparently *Persian* was the language employed. A certain degree of almost friendly intercourse between the two belligerents seems suggested by the fact that, on one occasion at any rate, an amicable conversation took place outside the walls of the fortress between a native "captain of the gate" and one of our officers. And, when the Rajah of Bhurtpoor (Doorjun Saul) learned that his followers had killed and then mutilated a British soldier, whom they had taken prisoner in the neighbouring jungle, we are told that "he sternly rebuked the perpetrators of this dastardly act."[1]

[1] "So exasperated were the men of the European regiments on hearing of the fate of their comrade, that previous to the assault they took a solemn oath over a dram of spirits to spare neither man, woman, nor child,

The mining operations continued to be pressed on incessantly, until their work was done. On the 12th of January, the two chief points of attack, the north-east angle of the fort and the "long-necked" bastion that faced General Nicholls's position, were each commenced upon. "On the 16th, two mines exploded in the long-necked bastion, brought down the thick outer casing of clay, and exposed and partly destroyed the brick core of the bastion on which the guns had rested. The guns came down with the mass of clay, and in a very short time our artillery demolished and finished the brick core. Next morning we found the breach partially repaired with large logs of wood, trunks of trees, and clay; but before night these repairs were destroyed by our batteries."[1] "On the 17th, the mine under the angle

when they took the place." Which was, no doubt, a very chivalrous and heroic resolve. The *Memoirs* state, at the same place (vol. ii. p. 76): "It is asserted, though without any proof, that they kept their word."

[1] *From Cadet to Colonel.*

of the north-east bastion, or cavalier, as it was termed, having been completed, was charged with ten thousand pounds of powder —with one exception, the largest charge ever used by our engineers—and had a train of three hundred feet leading under the ditch."[1] This mine was intended to make the chief breach in the walls of Bhurtpoor, and it was to be sprung on the following day, simultaneously with two others. The explosion of these mines was to be the signal for the general assault.

The plan of attack, briefly stated, was this. On our extreme right, or the northern side of the town, a detachment under Colonel Delamain was to force an entrance by the breach previously made by our artillery on the west side of the Jungeenah Gate.[2] To render this breach more accessible, a mine (one of the

[1] *Memoirs*, vol. ii. p. 95.

[2] The position of Colonel Delamain's force will be seen by a reference to Captain Field's sketch, and to the plan; the Jungeenah Gate (though not visible in the

two subordinate mines just referred to) had been duly laid, and was to be sprung just before the assault.

The main column [1] was that under General Reynell, who acted immediately under the eye of the Commander-in-Chief, and his assault was to be delivered against the north-east, or Pathan bastion. It is this attack that forms the foreground of Captain Field's picture (and is marked "B" on the plan.)

General Nicholls's command was of almost

picture) being on the hither side of these troops. This picture of the Storming of Bhurtpoor is a reduced copy of a coloured lithograph, "printed and published at the Asiatic Lithographic Press, Park Street, Chowringhee, Calcutta, 1827." The original sketch was "drawn on the spot by Captain G. E. F. Field," and, if it is not highly artistic, may be accepted as a faithful rendering of the scene. The colouring of the original lithograph has been reproduced in this miniature copy. The only liberty I have taken with the picture is the addition of notes explaining the four separate assaults; and the portraiture tallies so closely with the written description and the plan in Lord Combermere's *Memoirs* that there is hardly room for error in these notes.

[1] Of which Delamain's force was a detachment.

equal importance to that of Reynell. His forces were to advance against the famous "long-necked" bastion, but on entering the moat, a detachment under Colonel Wilson was to turn to the right, and to carry by escalade an outwork (marked "C" on the plan). Nicholls's main force was to gain an entrance through the breach in the "long-necked" bastion, which had been made by the mine sprung on the 16th. This assault, as well as Colonel Wilson's, is delineated in the picture (and is marked "D" on the plan). A subsidiary portion of Nicholls's column was also to attack the gun-breach on our extreme left (at the point marked "E" on the plan, which, in the picture, is hidden from view by the "long-necked" bastion).

Thus the end was at hand. The explosion of the 16th had cleared the way for Nicholls, and the other three mines were ready to be fired.

All the necessary instructions had been given by the night of the 17th, and due care was taken to prevent the besieged from apprehending that the crisis was reached. In silence and darkness, the storming-parties filed into the trenches at an early hour on the morning of the 18th; and when day broke every man was in his place, though not visible to the enemy—strict orders having been given that not a head nor a weapon should be allowed to project from the shelter of the parapets. We are told by Seaton that these precautions were successful, and that the garrison had no idea an assault was imminent; but in the *Memoirs* we read that our designs were suspected (perhaps reported by spies), in evidence of which a heavy fire was opened from the battlements at daybreak, lasting, with little intermission, until about eight o'clock in the morning. This was only replied to by our batteries, the stormers remaining passively hidden in the trenches. Shortly after eight o'clock, the announcement was made that all was ready.

As already stated, the explosion of the

three mines was the pre-arranged signal for the general assault. The principal mine was to shatter the front of the Pathan bastion; and of the two lesser mines, one had been laid so as to widen the breach near the Jungeenah Gate, while the other was to blow in the counterscarp on the west side of the north-eastern angle. These two mines were the first to be sprung; and their explosion brought the startled garrison to the walls of the north-east bastion. These—eight hundred Pathan warriors—were now seen, "dressed either in white or brightly coloured garments, some waving their swords in defiance, others beckoning eagerly for support." It was under their bastion that the great mine had been laid, and the stormers hung back for the explosion of those ten thousand pounds of powder. The pause was brief. Suddenly, the front of the bastion heaved, the ground below trembled as with an earthquake, and then, with a dull, heavy roar, "up went the mine, throwing high into the air heads, legs, and arms, blocks of timber, and masses of masonry and clay, enveloping all that part of the town and trenches with a thick cloud of smoke and dust." With that portion of the bastion, three hundred of its brave defenders had been torn into fragments.

The falling *débris* had killed or wounded a score of men in our trenches, also; but, as soon as the momentary cloud of smoke and dust that overhung them had cleared away, the troops of the main column rushed forward to the breach, amid the cheers of their comrades. Immediately afterwards, fired with the example thus set to them, and without waiting for the word of command, the troops under Nicholls sprang out of the trenches, and, in the midst of a terrible storm of grape and musketry that burst from the ramparts, and from "those huge mud mounds of the citadel," dashed across the open ground and up into the breach made in the "long-necked" bastion.

As Reynell's leading brigade[1] struggled stubbornly up the shattered bastion, stumbling over stones and clods and the mangled bodies of their foes, the incessant volleys from the battlements struck down many of their number. But they pressed bravely on, and in a few minutes the regimental colours of the 14th were waving from the summit. The point, however, was not yet won. For now the valiant men who garrisoned this bastion, recovering from the shock and confusion of this sudden and destructive outburst, rushed fiercely against the invaders. So stern and resolute was their defence, that of the five hundred men who met our attack on this bastion, only *seventy* were alive when the struggle was over. Driven slowly backward by the advancing bayonets of the British, they contested every available point, "their gunners particularly fighting with such devo-

[1] "Composed of four companies of H.M.'s 14th Regiment, the 58th Native Infantry, and one hundred Ghoorkas of the Nusseeree battalion."

tion that at the close of the day they were found almost to a man lying dead, with their swords still firmly grasped, round the guns they had so well served." But our troops—British, Sepoys, and Ghoorkas—pressed irresistibly on, driving them along the ramparts to the right.

Reynell's second brigade, led by Major Bishop (the first was led by Major Everard),[1] had followed close on the heels of the first. And as the first brigade had, according to the pre-arranged plan, turned to the right hand, on gaining the summit, so did the second brigade fight their way towards the left. Here they had work to do in silencing an outwork from which a telling fire was being directed upon the left main column, under Nicholls, then ascending the steep breach in the face of the "long-necked" bastion.

[1] Both of these brigades were deprived of their commanding officers at the outset, as Brigadier McCombe, of the first, and Brigadier Patton, of the second brigade, were struck down by the *dèbris* falling into the trenches after the explosion of the great mine.

Eventually, Major Bishop's forces became amalgamated with General Nicholls's division.

The outwork just spoken of was that which Colonel Wilson's party had been directed to take by escalade.[1] Here a small breach had been made by our guns, but the ascent was so abrupt that only Wilson and a few of his men gained the top (presumably, about the time of Bishop's arrival there), and the rest of his command turned back, and followed Nicholls's forces up the breach in the "long-necked" bastion.

In the face of a tremendous fire from ramparts and from citadel, the main body of Nicholls's column, led by Brigadier Edwards, had charged bravely up the breach, and although the ascent was steep, and many of their number were struck down as they

[1] Wilson's detachment was headed by pioneers carrying six ladders, made of bamboo, and "lined with stout canvas, stretched taut." Such ladders were used by other parties of the assailants, the steepness of the ascent rendering them necessary, especially at those points where the breaches had only been made by our artillery.

climbed, they maintained the most admirable discipline, not firing a shot until they reached the summit. In a few minutes they were masters of the bastion; and then, advancing rapidly along the "neck" that joined it to the ramparts, they forced the main body of their opponents to retreat down into the town by the connecting "ramp," the remainder being driven along the ramparts to the left. It was at this juncture that Major Bishop's forces effected a union with them. The assailants then pursued the enemy along the "terre-plein" to the left, but in doing so were subjected to a heavy fusillade from the adjoining houses, which thinned their ranks, and cost them the life of their brigadier (Edwards), with whom fell five other officers. But Nicholls's second brigade, under Fagan, had followed up the charge of the leading brigade, and, descending into the town, cleared the neighbouring houses of the musketeers, who were fusillading the right flank of the first brigade. And Nicholls's reserve brigade, under Adams, had entered the town by the Agra Gate,[1] and was now dispersing the enemy in the adjoining streets. The fortunes of the attacking party on Nicholls's extreme left are not followed by the writers of the *Memoirs*, but their success or failure was immaterial, since their comrades all around were everywhere driving the enemy before them.

The only other assault remaining to be noticed is that of Colonel Delamain's detach ment, directed against the breach on the west side of the Jungeenah Gate. It will be remembered that the mine beneath this breach was the first to be fired; and immediately afterwards Delamain led his men to the attack. In spite of a desperate opposition, he succeeded in forcing the enemy to retreat towards the Jungeenah Gate, where a terrible fate awaited them. Here a narrow street led

[1] There is no gate specially styled the "Agra Gate." Probably the Muttra Gate, on the left of Nicholls's position, which was presumably an exit for Agra, is the one thus denoted in the *Memoirs*.

from the gate into the town, but on a level lower than the adjoining ramparts by sixty feet. The only descent into this defile was by steep flights of steps. And just as the Jauts retreating before Delamain reached the western edge of this descent, those whom Everard and his column were driving before them had arrived at its *eastern* side. Standing at bay on either side of this chasm, the Jauts "fought with the fury of desperation; but our men were not to be withstood, and, first plunging their bayonets into the bodies of their opponents and then firing off their pieces, they pushed the hapless foe into the abyss below." "In about ten minutes the whole party, two hundred in number [Seaton says 'many hundreds'], lay wedged at the bottom of this awful gulf—a helpless, groaning, bleeding, burning mass." "The uniforms they wore being of cotton cloth, well padded with cotton wool, and quilted, these, as our men fired close, caught fire and burnt like tinder. Many, too, were set on fire by their own slow-matches. Altogether it was a terrible scene." Several brave attempts were made by our men to rescue them, a task rendered dangerous by the frequent explosions of their matchlocks and ammunition, while, in one instance, the rescuer was nearly killed by the man he was trying to save. A very few, "some three or four, less jammed in than the rest," were extricated, but the remainder were left to their fate.[1]

By this time Bhurtpoor was virtually in the hands of the British. The various storming-parties had captured every bastion, leaving in each, and at each gateway, a sufficient defensive force, while the others traversed the streets of the town. There was much street-fighting to do, and the enemy, still holding the larger brick houses in the town, succeeded in shooting down a considerable number of our men before they

[1] "Two hours later," says the *Memoirs*, "an officer of the staff repassed the same spot; he found nothing 'but a confused mass of burnt and burning bodies.'"

could be dislodged. A strong force still held the citadel, and until it could be captured our victory was not assured. The surrender of this stronghold, the same afternoon, is thus described to us in Combermere's *Memoirs*:—

"After mounting the breach as described,[1] Lord Combermere and his staff proceeded to the Jungeenah Gate. From thence, after rescuing a few of the poor wretches who lay there roasting in their smouldering garments, and receiving intelligence of the success of the right column, he entered the town, and came out on the glacis of the citadel just after the death of Khoosial Singh and the slaughter of his followers.[2] Hearing that a white flag had

[1] The Commander-in-Chief had accompanied Reynell's troops up the breach in the Pathan bastion.

[2] "Major Hunter, 41st Native Infantry, at the head of some Sepoys and Europeans," had, a short time previously, followed up some of the retreating foe to the gate of the citadel. "In their terror and confusion, the garrison shut the gate before about a hundred of the fugitives could enter. Among these was Khoosial Singh, brother-in-law of Doorjun Sal [the defender of Bhurtpoor], and warmly devoted to his fortunes. Major Hunter advanced a few paces in front of his men and offered him quarter; when, with warlike fury, Khoosial

been hoisted, he sent Captain Macan, Persian interpreter, up to the gate of the citadel to parley. Receiving no answer, he dispatched an aide-de-camp to bring up two twelve-pounders. In the meantime, some of our field-guns, which had been dragged up to the breach, opened fire from the ramparts on the citadel, sending their shot into it with great precision. About three p.m. the two twelve-pounders had arrived, and everything was prepared for blowing in the gate, when a deputation came out with an offer of unconditional surrender. Lord Combermere sent for a battalion—he had only scattered detachments with him—to take possession of the citadel. This reinforcement arrived, when, all firing having ceased from the citadel, and not a sound or a man being seen within, an attempt was made to find some one to open the gate. For some time not an answer could be obtained; at length one or two men appeared, and by a mixture of cajoling and threatening were induced to open

Singh replied to the speaker with a terrific blow. Major Hunter put up his scabbard as a guard; but such was the stoutness of arm of the gallant Jal [read Ját], so great the sharpness of his sword, that the scabbard was cut through as if it had been paper, and Major Hunter's left arm nearly severed. Our men then rushed on Khoosial Singh, who fell pierced with innumerable bayonet-wounds, and with him died, in a few minutes, nearly the whole of his band" (*Memoirs*, vol. ii. p. 118).

the first gate, which stands in a quadrangular stonework,[1] with turrets at the angles. From this gate a bridge led across the moat—which had then twenty-five feet of water in it—to a second gate, in the citadel itself. This gate was also locked; but the man who had opened the first entrance climbed up near to the top, and then, squeezing his body through an opening—for the gate did not shut quite close—descended on the inside, and gave admittance to our troops, who at once hoisted the king's colour of the 37th Native Infantry, at sight of which a universal shout of triumph burst from every one who beheld it. A regiment of Native Infantry was left as a garrison, and Lord Combermere returned to camp."

Some hours before the British colours floated from the tower of the citadel, the occupants of the palace had fled. The *Memoirs* thus recount the fortunes of Doorjun Sāl, at this crisis:—

"That prince, finding, between ten and twelve o'clock, that the fortune of the day was going against him, hastened to the citadel for his wife and family. Collecting a vast amount of treasure,

[1] Delineated in plan.

and taking with him his wife and two sons, and followed by a picked band of forty chosen horsemen, he resolved to cut his way out. At the Kombheer Gate he encountered a small picket of H.M.'s 14th, on whom his party fell fiercely, wounding six or eight, and thus opening a pathway for their master. Keeping close under the city walls for some distance, he entered a thick jungle, where he was joined by some more of his horsemen. He now spent some two hours in this jungle, seeking in vain an opportunity to escape, for every outlet from the place was well watched by our cavalry. At length, about half-past two, Brigadier Sleigh, having captured six or seven thousand fugitives, and seeing no more coming out of the town, dismissed the brigade. The men had scarcely dismounted, when the riding-master of the 8th Light Cavalry reported that there was a body of the enemy's cavalry in front. Lieutenant Barbor was ordered to mount his troop and gallop after a small body to the left, Colonel Gill, with the remainder of the regiment, pursuing a larger force which was making off on the right. Lieutenant Barbor soon came up with the smaller body, and, accosting one of the party, who seemed from his dress to be a chieftain of rank, demanded his sword. This was peremptorily refused, and Barbor, drawing his pistol, declared he would shoot him if he resisted. The pistol was cocked, levelled, Barbor's finger was on the trigger, and in another instant Doorjun Sal would have been a corpse, when some one exclaimed that it was the rajah. On this, Barbor returned his pistol, and Doorjun Sal, seeing the uselessness of further resistance, gave up his sword. With him were also captured his wife and his eldest son, a boy ten years old, who, riding behind a horseman, had a finger broken by a pistol-bullet in the momentary *mêlée* which had taken place. The other son, a child five years of age, was carried off by a faithful adherent and escaped. Each of the horsemen who accompanied Doorjun Sal had from 1200 to 2000 gold mohurs—equivalent to from £1920 to £3200—sewn up in the lining of his saddle."

Next morning, the British general and his staff breakfasted in the hall of the rajah's palace, "a regimental band playing 'God save the King' in honour of the occasion." During the next few days, the outlying forts, and the rest of the territory of Bhurtpoor, were completely subjugated by the British, and peace was restored. On the fifth of February, the rightful heir to the throne (the young son of the late rajah, Baldeo

Singh), was formally proclaimed Rajah of Bhurtpoor by the British officials; although the honours he succeeded to were sadly shorn of their former splendour, his kingship being now entirely dependent upon the will of the British Empire, which had also appropriated about £500,000 of the property of its ward. On the 6th of February, the fortifications of Bhurtpoor were blown up, and "the army was marched towards the frontiers of Alwar." The usurping rajah, Doorjun Saul, was sent as a prisoner to Benares. Of his garrison of twenty-five thousand men, it is said that there were thirteen thousand killed and wounded during the siege, four thousand of these being slain in the grand assault; and, of their armaments, "two guns and 133 pieces of ordnance fell into our hands," not to mention the lesser spoils. Out of the besieging force of something like twenty-nine thousand men, the total loss only amounted to between ten and eleven hundred.

The people of Bhurtpoor seem to have "accepted the situation" with great equanimity; no doubt, recognizing that they had been fairly conquered, and that the victors were wonderfully lenient. Probably, too, they had had enough of the agonies of war. When Lord Combermere paid a brief visit to Bhurtpoor in 1828, its appearance and the attitude of the people formed a strong contrast to the state of things described in the foregoing pages. "Though only two years had elapsed since the siege, the place, with the exception of the fortifications, presented few signs of the fearful bombardment under which it had suffered. The inhabitants seemed to have recovered their former prosperity, and were even cordial in the reception they gave their conqueror;" in whose honour a dinner was given by the young rajah. And when Sir William Gomm, the then Commander-in-Chief of India, wrote from Bhurtpoor, in 1851, to Lord Combermere, his letter contained such remarks as these: "The rajah is doing all sorts of kind things to oblige and amuse us. . . . We move to-morrow towards Deeg, the rajah insisting on accompanying us in person out of his territory, and showing us some hawking by the way. . . . To-day we all dine at the palace, the rajah presiding in person."[1] That the rajah should feel well disposed to the British was, of course, natural; since, without us, he would never have occupied the throne. But the thirteen thousand who fell in the siege died in defending their city against foreign invasion, and it is astonishing that the struggle did not engender a lasting feeling of hatred against their successful foe. That some such feeling was latent among them when Sir William Gomm paid his visit to Bhurtpoor is almost certain; for when, some years later, at the crisis of 1857–58, the then rajah (loyal to his suzerain) supplied a detachment of his troops to aid in re-

[1] See vol. ii. of Combermere's *Memoirs*, pp. 154, 292, and 293.

pressing the Mutiny in that neighbourhood, these Jaut soldiers mutinied in their turn against the British officers who were temporarily placed over them, whom they compelled to resign their commands in order to save their lives. Nor is it to be wondered at that men of their race, some of whom were perhaps veterans of the siege, and all of whom were soldiers in a semi-independent army, should object to follow the lead of alien officers against people who were, in one sense, their fellow-countrymen.

But those old animosities are dying out, there is reason to believe, among the uneducated as well as among the educated classes in India. And none of the latter class in Bhurtpoor are likely to be of the opinion that its former condition was better than its present. They have still a small standing army, but they have no enemies except the enemies of the British Empire. Two or three generations ago, their chief towns had to be strongly fortified, to protect them from conquest or extermination by rival tribes. Nowadays, all their civilizing tendencies have free play, education is fostered throughout their state, and their material prosperity is greatly developed. With the railway and telegraph keeping them in touch with the whole civilized world, themselves belonging to one of its foremost divisions, it is not likely that the educated people of modern Bhurtpoor see anything to regret in the changed condition of things. As for the rights and wrongs of the struggle of sixty years ago, they may be left to take care of themselves. The conquest of the weaker by the stronger was not really regarded as a "wrong" by either side; but, at any rate, the British have done a good deal in the way of atonement for any of their acts that may have been unjustifiable. Nor, although the brave defenders of Bhurtpoor were ultimately defeated, is there anything humiliating in the recollection. Defeat is often as honourable as victory, and Bhurtpoor has little to be ashamed of in the story of its siege.

A not unnatural interest in the incidents of the struggle has led me to quote much more fully than I had intended from the works out of which my information has been taken. But everything bearing upon the manners and customs of the people of Bhurtpoor ought to be of interest to those who concern themselves with the subject of Professor De Goeje's treatise. For the people of the besieged city were, and are, mainly Jauts by blood, and therefore, according to one set of theorists, of gypsy descent. Consequently, when we gain a glimpse or two of Bhurtpoor customs, prior to British intervention, we are gaining some idea of the ways of the Jauts. To what extent the manners of Bhurtpoor, in 1825–26, were characteristic of the Jauts as a nation, is of course open to question. But one would think that where a proud and powerful family had maintained its independence for many generations, it would also have preserved, in a marked degree, many of its ancestral usages. A few such usages I shall briefly notice.

REMARKS ON CERTAIN GYPSY CHARACTERISTICS.

As soon as the fortress of Bhurtpoor had yielded to the assault of Combermere's army, he sent out a portion of his forces to scour the neighbouring territory, and thus prevent the fugitives from the city from joining with the provincials, and making a second stand at one or the other of the outlying strongholds. "Our brigade," says Colonel Seaton, "went round the district, and found the strong fort of Biana abandoned, as well as those of Weer and Combheer. On the walls of the fort at Weer we found some enormous iron guns, built up something in the style of our present Armstrongs, but with this difference, that over the inner core of longitudinal bars, forming the bore, iron hoops, not coils, were shrunk on, over which came a layer of longitudinal bars, welded on parallel to the bore, and outside these another layer of hoops shrunk on. The diameter of these guns at the muzzle was enormous—something like three feet, and the bore was small. I should suppose they were about 40-pounders. I don't think any amount of powder would have burst them. It is a marvel how they could have been forged. I never saw a native anvil anything so large as our common blacksmith's anvil. These guns are a curious instance of the large works successfully carried out by the natives of India with the rudest and simplest of means."

Most, if not all, of the cannon found in India, and believed to be of early date, are of this make. So, indeed, are all primitive cannon. "The earliest cannon were not cast," says Mr. Paul Bataillard;[1] "they were made of iron bars, bound together and con-

[1] Quoting from Delon, *Le cuivre et le bronze.*

solidated like fasces, by iron hoops." Whether the expression "the earliest cannon" be held to apply to Europe or to Asia, this description is true.[1] But the use of artillery is of comparatively modern date in Europe, while Asia, and notably India, can claim an immemorial acquaintanceship with fire-arms. "Cannon and guns, or any kind of fire-arms," are referred to in certain Hindoo laws, which some authorities place as far back as the sixteenth century, B.C.;[2] and, presumably, they were in use before the era in which these laws were enacted. And it is believed, and very naturally, that artillery was introduced into Europe by people coming from India.

Now, if the "enormous iron guns," de-

[1] In England, cannon of this make "were gradually improved, but it was not until the reign of Henry VIII. that the founders succeeded in casting iron ordnance, to the entire exclusion, thenceforward, of cannon formed of square or rounded bars welded together." (*Chambers's Encyclopædia*, article "Fire-arms.")

[2] *Encyclopædia Britannica*, 9th edition, article "Gunpowder."

scribed by Seaton, were made by the Jauts themselves, and if this craft was one which they inherited from their ancestors, who were the earliest-known inhabitants of Sind, it is quite likely that the Indians who taught this knowledge to Europeans were of the race of the Jauts. This is almost equivalent (many would say wholly equivalent) to saying that the use of artillery was brought into Europe by gypsies.

Although Bataillard, so far as I am aware, does not go the length of saying this, he has nevertheless, some important remarks upon this point, to the following effect:—" I do not know whether the gypsies have been capable of casting or making cannon; but what is certain is that they have been known to *improvise*, on occasion, the manufacture of cannon-balls. Evidence is given of this, so early as 1496, by a mandate of that date granted by Wladislas, King of Hungary, wherein we learn that Thomas Polgar, chief of twenty-five tents of wandering gypsies, had, with his people, made at Fünfkirchen musket-balls and other ammunition for Bishop Sigismond. *En revanche*, when Mustapha, the Turkish governor of Bosnia, besieged the town of Crupa, in 1565, the Turks having exhausted their supplies of powder and shot, the gypsies were employed to make cannon-balls, some of iron, others of stone.[1] That gypsies could accomplish more difficult feats than these, if required to do so, I have no doubt. Like the Hindoo artificers, they produce wonderful effects with the rudest instruments.[2] One thing is certain, and it is of prime importance in the argument maintained by me, and that is, that before the manufacture of the implements of war had reached its later stages of development, they were the principal, if not

[1] The earliest cannon-balls, we are told, were made of stone.

[2] "These guns," says Colonel Seaton, in the passage quoted above, "are a curious instance of the large works successfully carried out by the natives of India with the rudest and simplest of means."

the only armourers, in certain countries of Eastern Europe. 'Formerly,' says Kogalnitchan, speaking of the gypsies of Roumania, 'it was they who were the makers of muskets, lances, swords, bomb-shells, and all the other arms required in war.'"[1]

The two dates here specially mentioned by Bataillard are of the fifteenth and sixteenth centuries. There are, of course, many instances of the use of artillery in Western Europe at earlier periods than these; but it is noteworthy that when the English were holding Boulogne against the French, in the year 1546, the English "Council at Boulogne" included in one of their despatches to the Privy Council in England the following statement:—"That the French King hath, by th' advice of two gentlemen of Hungary, very experient, made a great

[1] Bataillard's *Les Zlotars ou Dzvonkars*, pp. 531, 532 of the *Mémoires de la Société d'Anthropologie de Paris* (t. i. de la 2e série). These "Zlotars," or "Dzvonkars" (lit. *bell-makers*), are the gypsy artificers in bronze and brass-work in Eastern Galicia and the Bukovina.

number of cannons of a greater calibre than ever hath been seen; and determineth and advaunteth to beat this town all to powder."[1] That these two "very experient" master-gunners from Hungary were of the same race as those who furnished ammunition to Sigismond in 1496, and to the Turks in 1565, seems very likely, when one remembers that the gypsies were formerly "the principal, if not the only armourers in certain countries of Eastern Europe." If they were called "Hungarians" by the English and French, that would not affect this theory at all; because gypsies, like other immigrants, have usually been styled according to the nationality of the country whence they came (*e.g.*, *Bohemians* by the French) without further inquiry as to their special lineage. Assuming this belief to be correct, then,

[1] *Works of Henry Howard, Earl of Surrey, etc.*, edited by G. F. Nott, D.D., vol. i. p. 208. London, 1815. For this information (as for many other unacknowledged references) I am indebted to Mr. F. H. Groome.

these two "gentlemen of Hungary" would appear to denote that the Hungarian gypsies of the sixteenth century possessed a fuller knowledge of the art of fabricating artillery than the races of Western Europe.

These latter people, of course, had already possessed something of that knowledge. But there were gypsies in Western Europe before the sixteenth century. And they may reasonably be supposed to have brought with them this particular science, since it was known to their forefathers and kinsmen. We have a record of "how at Constantinople certain descendants of the race of Simon Magus, *Atsinkan* by name, sorcerers and famous rogues, slew wild beasts by their magic arts in the presence of Bagrat IV.," in the eleventh century.[1] And if these *Atsinkan* were, as is supposed, *Zingani* or gypsies, it is likely that it was their knowledge of the use of fire-arms which gave them this "magic" power. Those gypsy pirates who

[1] *Encyc. Brit.*, 9th edit., art. "Gipsies."

ascended the Tigris in the year 865,[1] carried, it may be remembered, three "firemen" in each barge, whose duty it was to attack the enemy with Greek fire, or some other combustible material. Possibly those "firemen" did not use gunpowder. But as they were "Indians," and as there had been laws passed in India, two thousand years before, against the use of "cannon and guns, or any kind of fire-arms," it does not seem at all improbable that they were armed with match-locks and "jingalls," or "jinjalls."[2]

Whatever may be thought of a theory which would identify the first use of fire-arms in Europe with the advent of the first

[1] See Appendix to Professor De Goeje's treatise, Note H.

[2] Although the former of these spellings is in agreement with our dictionaries, it may be noted that in Lord Combermere's *Memoirs* and Colonel Seaton's book, the word is spelt "jinjall," or "ginjal." The occurrence in different books, and on several occasions, of these spellings precludes the idea that they are not those originally given by the two writers, who, no doubt, had heard the word used times without number.

gypsy detachment, it is at least incontrovertible that when the British forces bombarded the fortifications of Bhurtpoor, their fire was answered by artillery of a much more primitive fashion, out of which their own modern weapons had been evolved.[1]

Other evidences of the high attainments in metal-working possessed by the Bhurtpoor Jauts may be seen in the finely-tempered chain-armour worn by their cavaliers; and by the keenness of their swords, which were so keen that a single blow from one of them,

[1] This applies to small-arms, as well as to cannon. The following extract from *Blackwood's Magazine* (Dec., 1885, p. 776) will help to render this apparent to those who have not considered the matter:—"The Crown Prince Rudolph, in his recent journal of a tour in the East, speaks of the Bedouins at the springs of Moses carrying primitive guns, 'with long cords twisted round them, which had to be lighted and let burn until they came in contact with the powder in the pan. . . .' This is an exact description of the matchlock carried by the English soldiers in 1677." The matchlock was otherwise known as a *fusee*, or *fusil;* from the French word, still in use. The term "firelock" probably dates from the same period as these.

dealt by a powerful arm, was sufficient to cut through a steel scabbard, "as if it had been paper," and to maim the arm which held the scabbard for the remainder of its owner's life.[1] It is probable that this proficiency in the manufacture of steel was also inherited from their forefathers.

Similar comments might also be made regarding their knowledge of fortification, the style of which is substantially the same as that of Europe. Other of their characteristic customs, such as the amusement of hawking, are also suggestive of our "romantic" period.[2]

[1] Major (afterwards General) Hunter is mentioned as thus disabled, in 1844, by the blow which he received from Khoosial Singh in 1826, at the gate of the citadel of Bhurtpoor. (Kaye's *Sepoy War*, 2nd edit. pp. 284, 285. London, 1865.)

[2] Captain Burton (in his *Falconry in the Valley of the Indus*. London, 1852) speaks of hawking as a notable feature among the customs of the races inhabiting the Indus Valley; and that it was a pastime of the Bhurtpoor Jauts is seen from the fact that this was among the amusements offered by the rajah to Sir William Gomm in 1851.

But enough has already been said upon these points.

In Professor De Goeje's account of the Jauts, their herds of buffaloes are frequently spoken of; and these accompanied the captive Jauts in their various deportations—to the fens of the Tigris and the Euphrates, to the frontiers of Syria, and, in the year 855, into the territory of the Byzantines.[1] This feature of Jaut life is commented upon in an interesting way by Mr. Bataillard,[2] who first quotes the following statement by Dr. Paspati :—

"To the west of Tchorlu (which lies about 70 miles north-west of Constantinople), there is a place of considerable size, called Hariupol (Charioupolis), or, according to the Turks, Hariampól and Herepoli, in which place there are many gypsies. These possess a large number of buffaloes, the best in Roumelia. It is their custom to start from

[1] See pp. 29, 30, of Professor De Goeje's account.

[2] See his Letter to the *Revue Critique* (Sept. 25, Oct. 2, and Oct. 9, 1875); pp. 10, 11, of the extracted publication (Paris, 1875).

Hariupol every spring, in waggons drawn by buffaloes; and, travelling along through the moist valleys, they continue the journey until all their animals are sold. Their families, and also their cooking utensils, are bestowed in the waggons. All of these gypsies are Musulmans, and most of them are rich. Their waggons usually number from five to ten. In the autumn, they return again to their winter-quarters at Hariupol; in which place there are 650 families, of whom 500 are Turks."

Mr. Bataillard then remarks: "If this passage be compared with that in which Mr. De Goeje describes the transportation to Antioch and Mopsuestia, in 714, of a certain number of Zotts and other Indians, *with their buffaloes, to the number of* 4000, . . . as also the later deportations of these same Zotts, and, finally, their introduction into the territory of the Byzantine Empire in the year 855, then there is every reason for supposing that, in the gypsies of Hariupol, we have an actual remnant, wonderfully well conserved, of these Zotts or Jatts. It would be most interesting to study them on the spot, to collect their traditions, and the ethnical names by which they designate themselves, as well as those which may be given to them by others in that neighbourhood, and to note all the details which may distinguish them from other gypsies, in respect to type, language, manners, and customs. The buffaloes themselves, however, are widely scattered, being found even in Roumania, where they are much valued for their milk. The Roumanian gypsies do not possess buffaloes; but in Roumania one falls in, at rare intervals, with some family of Roumelian gypsies, having along with them a buffalo-cow, whose milk affords them daily nourishment. In this region, therefore, there ought also to be some information obtainable."

In a recent number of the *Illustrated London News*,[1] there is an instructive drawing

[1] October 3, 1885.

by Mr. Caton Woodville, entitled "In the Plains of Roumelia," and there can be no doubt that the people who form the subject of the picture are some of these same gypsies. The foreground is almost wholly filled in by a heavy, clumsy cart, drawn by a pair of buffaloes, yoked together, and driven by a very gypsy-looking man, who, with his tawny wife and child, sits in the cart. Beside the stream (in which the oxen are standing) is a man of similar appearance; and, in the near background, another equipment, of like description, is coming up. So Oriental is the effect of all these figures, particularly of the man standing beside the stream, that had the picture been called "In the Plains of Sind," the name would have appeared almost, or quite, as suitable, to ordinary Europeans. If these, then, are the people referred to by Dr. Paspati (and it can hardly be otherwise), their whole characteristics point them out as almost certainly some of the descendants of Mr. De Goeje's Jauts of the ninth century.

Among the gypsies of Roumelia,[1] and of various parts of Turkey, is a certain subdivision called the *Zapáris*, or *Djapáris*. This caste is of special interest. Because Dr. Paspati, who refers to them as his "favourite gypsies,"[2] speaks of them as the least civilized of all the race.[3] Their expression is fierce, and their bearing proud; although they are regarded as belonging to the very lowest of Turkish gypsies, and are held in contempt by the Sedentary class. By blood and language, they declare themselves to be the purest specimen of the gypsy type in the Ottoman Empire, and to them also belong various songs and traditions that their more hybrid kinsmen appear to have forgotten.[4] The true gypsy, as represented by

[1] Presumably of Roumelia. See Bataillard's *Les Origines*, p. 32, note 1. 1876.

[2] "*Les Tchinghianés de ma prédilection*," p. 31.

[3] Pages 22 and 591.

[4] Paspati, pp. 13–15, 22, 31, and 591, 592. The description of those Zapáris (p. 31), when instructing their guest in the niceties of their language, reminds one

them, is described in these terms:—"His figure is erect, and wiry, his mien is savage, his complexion tawny, his hair black, and his eyes are black and glittering. He abhors his connections of the Sedentary class, and holds all house-dwellers in contempt."[1] These words are applied to the Nomad division in general, but Dr. Paspati clearly regards the Djapáris as the representative Nomads; so much so that one might say of them, *Grattez le Nomade et vous trouverez le Djapári.* It is from them that he has received the greater part of his vocabulary, and probably more than the greater part of his songs and tales. In speaking of them specially, Dr. Paspati employs words synonymous with those just given, adding such additional information as this: "They wear an enormous head-gear, and wide trousers. Their look is wild, their

strongly of our own English gypsies, as described by Mr. Crofton and others, and their eager desire that only "deep" Romanes should be communicated to the students of their speech.

[1] Page 14.

walk haughty. Three years ago, a band of these people, when strolling through the country about three hours' journey from Constantinople, killed two of the rural police who were making some rude remarks to their women. They nailed their victims down to the ground, by means of a piece of wood laid across their heads."[1]

Some of these Djapáris work as smiths during the winter months. But they are chiefly known as exhibitors of performing monkeys and bears, in which character they frequent fairs and the principal towns.[2] And this occupation at once suggests their connection with the Indian *Bediyás*, the *Multani* of Cabul, the Persian *Luris*, and certain gypsies of modern Egypt.[3] And a connection with

[1] Page 22.

[2] See Bataillard's *Les Origines*, p. 32, note, Paris, 1876; also Paspati, p. 22.

[3] See Appendix to Professor De Goeje's treatise, *ante*, pp. 82–84; also *ibid*, pp. 116–119 for their hypothetical connection with the earlier European exhibitors of apes and bears.

two, at any rate, of these divisions, the *Luris* and the *Multani*, means a connection with the Jauts of Sind.

One other trait of the Turkish gypsies that reminds one of the eastern Jauts, is afforded us by those abandoned daughters of the race, who are probably of the mixed "Sedentary" class, and "whom one meets in Constantinople and in the larger towns of the empire, singing in the streets, and beating time to their voices with loud clapping of the hands." These *Ghiovendé*, as they are called, are professional dancers and singers ("nautch girls," in short), and are generally such as Ursula Petulengro would have declined to name. Their manner of singing would, by itself, be a detail of too trifling an importance to mention here, but, taken in consideration with some of the other characteristics just noticed, it is not out of keeping with their assumed relationship to the Jaut soldiers whom Seaton saw amusing themselves in a similar fashion on the walls of Bhurtpoor.

MISCELLANEOUS REMARKS.

THERE seems no reason to doubt that the gypsies of the Ottoman Empire are largely the descendants of those Luris, or Jauts, who were brought westward from Sind, at various periods between the fifth and the ninth centuries. Indeed, those of them whose winter residence is at Tokát, in the province of Sivas, have a tradition that their forefathers came from Persia;[1] and they, accordingly, might be descended from the 12,000 sent to Behram Gour. Moreover, the term *sundò*, or *shundò*, which the Turkish gypsies apply to those of honourable estate, is identified by Dr. Paspati with the name *Sindo*, *Sinti*, or *Sindhi*, applied to certain

[1] Paspati, p. 17.

European gypsies.[1] This also points to the same origin. Whether the *Cascarots* of Saint-Jean-de-Luz have preserved in their name a reminiscence of the time when the Jauts inhabited the *Kaskar* plains, is more dubious.[2]

On the other hand, although many of the peculiarities which distinguish the Turkish gypsies suggest an Eastern origin at no very remote period, and although such an origin is very clearly marked out by Professor De Goeje, it is not necessary to believe that there had been no departure of *Luris* out of Sind until the days of Behram Gour. So far back as the times of Pindar and Herodotus, we have notices of Sindhis, Kerks, Meds, and (according to Bataillard) Zigani, settled on the north-eastern shores of the

[1] Paspati, p. 21.

[2] This similarity in name is pointed out in Bataillard's *Les Origines* (p. 7, note. Paris, 1875), though only as indicating what may *possibly* be a connection. These Cascarots are genuine gypsies (see Michel's *Le Pays Basque*, p. 144, note.[2] Paris, 1857).

Black Sea, and in the Danube regions.[1] The gypsies of modern Roumelia, and their buffaloes, may well be descended from those who entered the Byzantine Empire in the ninth century. But, nevertheless, their race may have been "Thracian" for a very much longer period than even a thousand years.

One thing clearly visible is, that those

[1] See Note E *ante*, pp. 66–70: also Bataillard's *L'origine des Tsiganes*, and his other works. I have further been directed to the following passages:—Strabo (book xi. p. 520), in some accounts of "those tribes which are perfectly barbarous, living about Mount Caucasus, and the other mountainous districts," states that "the Siginni in general practise Persian customs. They have small horses with shaggy hair, but which are not able to carry a rider." Rawlinson's *Herodotus* (vol. iii. p. 220) also states: "The only people I can hear of as dwelling beyond the Ister [the Danube] are the Sigynnæ, who wear, they say, a dress like the Medes, and have horses which are covered entirely with a coat of shaggy hair, five fingers in length. . . . Their borders reach down almost to the Eneti upon the Adriatic, and they call themselves colonists of the Medes." "The Sigynnæ of Europe," remarks Rawlinson, "are unknown to later historians and geographers. Apollonius Rhodius introduces them into his poem as dwelling upon the *Euxine*."

gypsies of the Ottoman Empire are distinctly Romané, like those of Europe. And, while the accounts of Paspati take us as far east as the banks of the Euphrates, other writers show us the Romané in countries more Eastern still. Mr. Leland, for example, makes the following statements :—[1]

"The Doms are a race of gypsies found from Central India to the far northern frontier, where a portion of their early ancestry appears as the Domarr, and are supposed to be pre-Aryan. . . . The Domarr are a mountain race, nomads, shepherds, and robbers. Travellers speak of them as 'gypsies.' A specimen which we have of their language would, with the exception of one word, which is probably an error of the transcriber, be intelligible to any English gypsy, and be called pure Romany. Finally, the ordinary Dom call himself a Dom, his wife a Domni, and the being a Dom, or the collective gypsydom, Domnipana. *D* in Hindustani is found as *r* in English gypsy speech—*e.g.* *doi*, a wooden spoon, is known in Europe as *roi.* Now, in common Romany we have, even in London—

Rom	A gypsy.
Romni	A gypsy wife.
Romnipen . . .	Gypsydom."

[1] *The Gypsies*, pp. 333, 334. 1882.

This Hindu word *dom* is recognized by Miklosich (*Beiträge*, iv. pp. 52, 53) as equal to *rom;* and Bataillard also remarks (*Les Origines*, p. 7, note [2]: 1875) that Pott, "in a passage which at this moment I cannot find, has noted an identification that was proposed to him between the gypsies and the *Dom*, a people seated at the base of the Himalayas, on the Indian side of the range. In support of this hypothesis, I might cite the name *Dumans*, borne by a tribe of Syrian gypsies, apparently of some importance (Newbold, *Journal of the R. Asiatic Society*, vol. xvi. part ii. p. 302, 303–307: Lond. 1856, 8vo), and the name *Doum* that the Syrian gypsies are said to give themselves (*ibid.*, p. 312). But, before basing a system of identification upon such comparisons," he remarks, in conclusion, "we ought to examine them more closely."

If, in addition to these statements, the evidence of Mr. Leland's "Mahometan Hindu from Calcutta"[1] is trustworthy, there are

[1] *The Gypsies*, p. 337. 1882.

nomadic *Roms* (thus called) all over India. The particular class of gypsies last spoken of are said, however, to be called "Syrians" by other people in India. Yet in spite of this, Mr. Leland's informant asserted that "they were full-blood Hindus, and not Syrians." "'Could he remember any of their words?' Yes. One of them was *manro*, which meant bread. Now, *manro* is all over Europe the gypsy word for bread. . . . These gypsies called themselves and their language *Rom*." The *Roms* to whom this Hindu refers may, however, be really the same as the *Doms* just spoken of. If the initial letter of the words *Doum* and *Duman* ought to be pronounced according to Hindu phonography, then the so-named Syrian gypsies of Newbold are most likely identical with Leland's *Roms*, or "Syrians." As the last-mentioned author remarks, these people may have been nothing more than temporary residents of Syria; and, although he appears to regard their assumed residence in that country as only a matter of a few years, it may actually have been of many centuries' duration, without affecting the case.

Be this as it may, it is clear that the Turkish gypsies are Romané. And so, apparently, are those of Persia. De Goeje, in speaking of the Persian gypsies, says "they still bear the name of Lûrî or Lûlî, applied to them long ago by Firdousi. Ouseley relates that they are well aware that their kinsmen are called Tchingâni by the Turks."[1] Moreover, he adds that "the name Lûrî does not properly belong to them," but is given to them by the Persians. Since, then, they recognize the Turkish gypsies as their *kinsmen*, it is to be inferred that the Persian "Lûrîs" are Romané, and speak a form of Romanes.

Now, Firdousi's "Lûrîs" are the "Jauts" of Hamza of Ispahan. Thus, the Jauts of ancient Sind, and of the modern countries of Afghanistan, Beloochistan, and India,

[1] De Goeje's "Contribution," *ante*, p. 41.

ought also to be Romané. Here, however, the linguistic test seems to fail. "Their language, now generally known as Sindhî, still bears the name of *Jat-kî-galî*, or Jat-language, in East Beloochistan and the Western Punjaub."[1] And, after comparing Captain Burton's specimens of this language with Romanes, Mr. Groome is of opinion that "in the face of the great unlikeness of Romani and Játakí," we ought not to regard the Jauts as Romané.[2]

On the other hand, while the language of these Jauts is so distantly related to that of the Romané, we have (on Mr. Leland's authority) an Indian gypsy race, the Doms (or Roms), with regard to whom he says: "A specimen which we have of their language would, with the exception of one word, which is probably an error of the transcriber, be intelligible to any English gypsy, and be called pure Romany."

[1] De Goeje's "Contribution," *ante*, pp. 37, 38.

[2] See Appendix, *ante*, pp. 81, 82.

From these statements, one is led to conjecture that the nominal Jauts of the present day are far from being pure descendants of the Jauts of the fifth century. And that those fifth-century Jauts are better represented by the Persian "Lûrîs" and the Turkish "Tchinghiané," and apparently also by the "Doms" or "Roms" of India. That, in short, the Jauts of Sind in the fifth century were genuine Romané, while the nominal Jauts of the present day are hybrids.

Yet it must be remembered that race and language may part company by reason of other causes than that of intermixture of blood. Without leaving the subject in question, we see this illustrated. Mr. De Goeje states that the Jauts and the Nawar of Syria were the same people.[1] And Mr. Leland (quoting Seetzen) says of gypsies: "The Turks call them Tschinganih; but the Syrians and Egyptians, as well as themselves, *Nury*, in the plural *El Naûar*." Of the list of

[1] See De Goeje's "Contribution," *ante*, p. 6.

words from this Nawar language supplied by Captain Newbold, Mr. Leland declares that it "does not contain a single word which would be recognized as Rommany."[1] Here, then, we have a race of people alleged to be Romané by blood, but whose language is very far removed from Romanes. The gypsies of Montenegro, who (we are told by Mr. Groome) have also lost the language of their race, furnish a like example.

The question of modern Indian gypsydom can only, however, be answered by oriental scholars. And only a passing reference can be made in these pages to other tribes of so-called gypsies, at present existing in India and in Ceylon; such as those known in Southern India as Weddahs or Veddahs, Nuts, Ruraver, Sámbádi, Ruruneru, and Sikáter, all of which tribes are classed by Dr. Mitra with the Bediyás (with a reservation as to those of Ceylon). The same authority also speaks of the Shidgárshids of

[1] See Leland's *English Gipsies*, 1874, pp. 194, 199.

the Dekhan as evidently a division of the Weddahs; while the Bunjáras of Central India, and the Konjis and Dombarus are referred to as possible gypsies. Those Dombarus, or Dumbaru, are mentioned by Mr. Lucas, author of *The Yetholm History of the Gypsies;* and probably the Konjis are the same as the Kanjars, or Kunjuras, with regard to whom, and the Dombarus, he makes some interesting remarks.[1] Mr. Lucas also states, on Captain Richardson's authority, that the Kunjuras are no other than those "Bazeegurs or Nuts" who inhabit "the upper provinces of Hindustan."

Dr. Mitra's account of "The Gypsies of Bengal,"[2] since it expresses the opinions and experiences of a gentleman of Indian birth and descent, is both interesting and valuable. But if language is to be the test of race, it cannot be said that his Bediyás, "the gypsies

[1] *Yetholm Gypsies*, pp. 88–91. 1882.

[2] *Memoirs of the Anthropological Society of London*, vol. iii. pp. 120–133. London, 1870.

of Bengal," are Romané. Indeed, as "the main principle of their language" is stated to be that exemplified by our costermongers' "back-slang;" and as the language so inverted is chiefly, perhaps wholly, Bengali; and as, moreover, "the grammatical construction of the Bediyá language is the same as that of the Bengali,"—it does not appear that "the gypsies of Bengal" actually possess a separate form of speech. Among those words which they pronounce in the correct fashion, no doubt many could be called "Romanes;" such as *pání* (water), *a'* (come), *ba'* (sit), *ja'* (go), *sui* (sleep). But then, these are also Bengali or Hindustani. One of their words, however, *chiti* (a crowbar), is identified by Mr. Groome with the Scotch-Gypsy *chittie* (an iron kettle-prop), and it may be that their vocabulary preserves other suggestive words. In some instances, what we should call "gypsy" words are found in the Bengali-Hindustani list alone; while the so-called "Bengal-Gypsy" equivalents are quite different. For example, in the former list one sees *mas* (flesh) and *chhuri* (knife), where the Bediyá list gives *guli* and *pándi*.

Of the characteristics and habits of the Bediyás, it may be noted that they are "a nation of thieves," and that they, like the Thugs,[1] "worship the goddess Kálí," who "is supposed to be the patroness of rogues and thieves." The Bediyás have their own chiefs and councils, whose decisions are implicitly obeyed, without any thought of an appeal to the recognized authorities of the land. In enumerating the well-known occupations of European gypsies, Dr. Mitra remarks, "The Bediyá in Bengal is ignorant

[1] Another suggestion of a connection between Thugs and gypsies is seen in the comparison which Mr. Groome makes between the *pola* of the Thugs and the *patteran*, or *patrin* of the Romané. For a description of the *pola*, he refers us to *Ramaseeana; or, a Vocabulary of the Thugs* (Calcutta: G. H. Huttmann, 1836), and the name of the vocabulary is itself rather suggestive. It may also be added that "at least 500 Bediyás are annually convicted of theft, housebreaking, and dacoity, in three or four districts of Bengal."

of none of these professions. In lying, thieving, and knavery, he is not a whit inferior to his brother of Europe, and he practises everything that enables him to pass an easy, idle life, without submitting to any law of civilized government, or the amenities of social life." "When in the neighbourhood of towns or villages," we are further told, "the Bediyá earns his livelihood by thieving, exposing dancing monkeys, bears, and serpents, retailing herbs, weaving baskets, and selling birds, squirrels, sheep, goats, and mungooses. When away from the habitation of civilized man, he is a hunter of jackals and foxes, a bird-catcher, a collector of herbs and simples. The Luri of Persia and the Multani of Cabul keep bears and monkeys,[1]

[1] "The Syrian gypsies, or Nuri, who are seen with bears and monkeys in Cairo, are strangers in the land. With them a conversation is not difficult" (Leland's *Gypsies*, p. 302). The Syrian gypsies and those of Egypt are so interlinked with the gypsies of India, that it may be permissible to quote still further from Mr. Leland's writings.

"There are three kinds of gypsies in Egypt—the

and all three are attended by wild, half-savage dogs, as are the Bunjáras of Central India and the gypsies of Europe." "The female Bediyá, or Bediyáni, is the very counterpart of her European sister. . . . Palmistry is her special vocation." She is also described as carrying with her a bundle of herbs, and other real or pretended charms against sickness of body and of mind; and she is much sought after by village maidens, for the sake of the philters with which she restores to them their estranged lovers; while

Rhagarin, the Helebis, and the Nauar. They have secret jargons among themselves; but as I ascertained subsequently from specimens given by Captain Newbold and Seetzen, as quoted by Pott, their language is made up of Arabic 'back-slang,' Turkish, and Greek, with a very little Romany." Of the Rhagarin, who call themselves "Tatâren," it is said: "Their women tell fortunes, tattoo, and sell small wares; the men work in iron (*quincaillerie*). They are all adroit thieves, and noted as such. The men may sometimes be seen going around the country with monkeys; in fact, they appear to be in all respects the same people as the gipsies of Europe" (Leland's *English Gipsies*, ch. x. 1874; *The Gypsies*, pp. 288–303, 1882).

she also makes the most daring forecasts, not only as to the date of an absent friend's return, but even as to the sex of unborn children. They are said, also, to interpret dreams, and, indeed, to practise all the arts of the European sibyl. Like the gypsy women of Cairo (*vide* Leland), they practise tattooing—"an art unknown to all in Bengal, except the Bediyánís." "Young girls are their principal patrons, and they generally get themselves tattooed between the eyebrows or below the under lip. Sometimes the breasts and the forearms are also subjected to the operation."

"The Bediyás show no tendency to obesity, and are noted for a light, elastic, wiry make, very uncommon in the people of this country [Bengal]. In agility and hardihood they stand unrivalled. The men are of a brownish colour, like the bulk of Bengalies, but never black. The women are of a lighter complexion, and generally well formed—some of them have considerable claims to beauty; and for a race so rude and primitive in their habits as the Bediyás are, there is a sharpness in the features of their women which we see in no other aboriginal race in India. Like the gypsies of Europe, they are noted for the symmetry of their limbs; but their offensive habits, dirty clothing, and filthy professions, give them a repulsive appearance, which is heightened by the reputation they have of kidnapping children, and frequenting burial-grounds and places of cremation. Their eyes and hair are always black, but their stature varies very much in different individuals." Dr. Mitra, however, here interposes a caution against assuming all nominal Bediyás to be really of that race. It seems there are, in Bengal, "a great number of men who profess to be Bediyás, but who turn out, on cross-examination, to be either outcasts or descendants of outcasts, who, for want of better, have adopted the profession of the Bediyás. . . . These, as well as other pseudo-Bediyás, have none of the physical peculiarities of their namesake, and are generally of a black complexion. Though popularly known as Bediyás, they keep distinct, and are never allowed to mix and intermarry with the true Bediyá."

"The true Bediyá does not often build a permanent house, and seldom takes to agriculture. . . . The place of their encampment is the outskirts of a village, and there they put up, with the mats and sticks, a few miserable little wigwams, in which men, women, and children huddle together, with little attention to ease or convenience. In some parts of the Burdwan and Baraset districts in Bengal, the Bediyás have permanent huts, like those of the native peasantry. They are frequently forsaken, and are put up only to evade the persecution of police officers."

"The dress of the Bediyás assimilates generally with that of the people among whom they live. The Nuts have party-coloured cloths hanging from different parts of their body, and jugglers sometimes put on some outlandish garment or other; but the great bulk dress very much in the same way as the natives of the country."

Dr. Mitra regards the Shidgárshids and the Weddahs (of whom they are a subdivision) as "the counterpart" of the Bediyás. They are, he says, quoting Mr. Stevenson, "a tribe of jugglers and fortune-tellers who wander about the Dekhan, and probably other parts of the country, where, however, they are not known by this name, but generally, we believe, by that of 'gorode' (juggler), which is the denomination of the caste in the *Vijñáneswara Sástra.* The Karnátaka term of 'shudgárshid' is derived from *shudgár* (a burning or burial ground), and *shid* (proficient, ready), it being their habit to prowl about these places to collect certain pieces of human bone with which they are supposed to work charms and incantations. The tribe is looked upon with much awe and detestation, and the fear of exciting the wrath of any of its members generally secures a ready compliance with their demands for charity. On this, however, they do not place their only reliance; they are notorious for kidnapping children, and also for an abominable traffic, consisting in the sale of sinews extracted from the breasts, the wrists, and the ankles of females. . . . The deity which they conceive chiefly entitled to their worship is the goddess Chowdhi (Chandi ?), whose principal shrine is in Malabar, where, we understand, the caste is most numerous. North of the Krishna they worship Rámástick, a goddess whose chief pagoda is in Kundáhár."

The word whence the Bengali form Bediyá comes is said by Dr. Mitra to be *Bede*, which he connects with a name given to gypsies or "Tartars" "before the time of Zinghis Khan." The "Tartars" he speaks of are the Romané of Northern Europe, known in the Scandinavian countries as "Tartars."

But it is not clear that Mitra's Bediyás and their compeers ought to be regarded as closely allied to the Romané. However, they cannot be left out in any consideration of the gypsies of India.

INDEX.

A

B

C

D

E

F

G

H

I

J

K

L

M

N

O

P

R

S

T

W

Y

Z